"*Abuelita Faith* offers a master class for those seeking liberation at the intersection of their own stories and Scripture. Many books explore theology, but very few offer such an expansive picture of God told through the eyes and stories of overlooked people. This book invites all of us to greater liberation through finding ourselves in God's story—the story of our ancestors who showed up and made a way for us."

—**Brandi Miller**, host, *Reclaiming My Theology* podcast

"*Abuelita Faith* does something few writings are able to do. It gives us back our memories of God in the places that matter the most: our homes and bodies. Thinking, sensing, doing, and loving in the name of God have become white, male, rational, normative operations in the Western space. But Armas has found God operating powerfully in the underside of academia, the church, and the city—that is, at home, through the wisdom and practice of mujeres luchadoras (women in the struggle) and life givers, true teachers of the Spirit. Armas combines the best of postcolonial theories with biblically informed and ethically reconstructive approaches to everyday life. A must-read for those of us wishing for a different way of doing theology and faith."

—**Oscar García-Johnson**, professor, Fuller Theological Seminary; author of *Spirit Outside the Gate: Decolonial Pneumatologies of the American Global South*

"*Abuelita Faith* is a celebration of women as genuine sources of theology. Leading from her experience as the daughter of Cuban immigrants, Armas shows us how the personal and biblical narratives of everyday women are essential to living unfragmented realities of life and faith. This is a book for churches, seminaries, men, and women."

—**Michelle Ami Reyes**, vice president, Asian American Christian Collaborative; author of *Becoming All Things: How Small Changes Lead to Lasting Connections across Cultures*

"With this stunning debut, Armas makes her mark as one of the most brilliant biblical scholars of her generation. Her beautiful and accessible prose brims with hope as she advocates for the marginalized and oppressed women in the biblical text with nuanced and original interpretations. Readers will encounter the liberative power

D0291405

of wrestling with the biblical text while they plumb the depths of the riches of Latinas' wisdom traditions. I am deeply grateful for all the ways Armas has offered me gentle encouragement to see my ancestresses anew. Her voice is an important one for our time."

—**Karen González**, theologian, immigration advocate, and author of *The God Who Sees*

"*Abuelita Faith* is perfectly named. Armas presents the traumatic history of the spirituality of marginalized women in a tender invitation as gentle as a grandmother setting a table. Like all good food, this book is meant to nourish—not only to open us to the lived experience of 'others' but to find in their witness a sustaining grace. Armas's delicate blend of history, experience, theology, and Scripture offers a rich meal that feeds our decolonization and reconstruction of Christian faith long after the last plate."

—**Emmy Kegler**, author of *One Coin Found: How God's Love Stretches to the Margins*

"In inspiring prose of metaphorical flor y canto (flower and song), Armas honors the spiritual dignity of our abuelas, mothers, and aunts, who are the unsung spiritual heroes of our Latine families. In the stories of women from sacred Scripture, she unearths the themes of their lessons and uplifts the abuelita faith that has shaped the Brown church for centuries."

—**Robert Chao Romero**, associate professor, César E. Chávez Department of Chicana/o and Central American Studies, UCLA; author of *Brown Church*

"The combination of surgical scholarship and poetic storytelling makes this book a treasure and a healing balm for those of us trying to imagine a way forward in our faith."

—**Sandra Maria Van Opstal**, executive director, Chasing Justice

"Reading *Abuelita Faith* is like feasting on a faith prepared by generations. Through incisive cultural commentary, beautifully written memories of family, and the retelling of biblical narratives, Armas invites us into a faith that is relational and embodied."

—**Hillary L. McBride**, psychologist, author, speaker, podcaster

"Armas brilliantly weaves together Scripture, theology, history, post-colonial and feminist scholarship, personal experience, and culture to demonstrate that powerful named and unnamed women fill not only the Bible but also our lives. These women, including our abuelitas and other mentors, are theologians, teachers, and activists who embody the wise and loving way of Christ. Overlooking and underappreciating them impoverishes us and the world. *Abuelita Faith* is compelling, sharp, inspiring. I anxiously look forward to reading whatever else Armas publishes!"

—**Marlena Graves**, author of *The Way Up Is Down: Becoming Yourself by Forgetting Yourself*

"As Armas tells of her own personal and communal formation under her abuela's gutsy, loving, and resistant spiritual life, she also carefully analyzes Scripture and evokes a tantalizing humanness in communion with God, family, and the world. *Abuelita Faith* is not an abstraction, an ideal, or an ideology; it's a challenging witness to a vigorously embodied hope."

—**Mark Labberton**, president, Fuller Theological Seminary

"Sometimes I read and have to tell someone about it. Other times I read, and it makes me sit, feel, think, reread, and pause. Armas's *Abuelita Faith* does just that—it's a theological miracle. Her words dance and sing in ways that made me rethink what it means to dance and sing and write as a theologian. This story, these words, this type of love, is the path to our liberation."

—**Dante Stewart**, writer and speaker

"Armas invites us to attend the weekly game of dominoes, sit with her family, hear their stories, and make and create together with familia. She weaves together the wisdom of her ancestors with the stories of women in Scripture, providing insights into how to survive and thrive in one's faith. Pastors, educators, and those trying to make sense of their own stories in light of the biblical story need this book."

—**Patrick B. Reyes**, award-winning Chicano author of *The Purpose Gap* and *Nobody Cries When We Die*

Abuelita *Faith*

What Women on the Margins
Teach Us about Wisdom,
Persistence, and Strength

Kat Armas

BrazosPress

a division of Baker Publishing Group
Grand Rapids, Michigan

Published by Brazos Press
a division of Baker Publishing Group
PO Box 6287, Grand Rapids, MI 49516-6287
www.brazospress.com

Printed in the United States of America

Library of Congress Cataloging-in-Publication Data
Names: Armas, Kat, 1989– author.
Title: Abuelita faith : what women on the margins teach us about wisdom, persistence, and strength / Kat Armas.
Description: Grand Rapids, Michigan : Brazos Press, a division of Baker Publishing Group, [2021] | Includes bibliographical references.
Identifiers: LCCN 2020052198 (print) | LCCN 2020052199 (ebook) | ISBN 9781587435089 (paperback) | ISBN 9781587435300 (casebound) | ISBN 9781493431113 (ebook)
Subjects: LCSH: Women in Christianity. | Christian women—Religious life.
Classification: LCC BV639.W7 A76 2021 (print) | LCC BV639.W7 (ebook) | DDC 248.8/43—dc23
LC record available at https://lccn.loc.gov/2020052198
LC ebook record available at https://lccn.loc.gov/2020052199

Some names and details of the people and situations described in this book have been changed or presented in composite form in order to ensure the privacy of those with whom the author has worked.

Published in association with Books & Such Literary Management, www.booksandsuch.com

21 22 23 24 25 26 27   7 6 5 4 3 2 1

Dedicado a mi abuela, Evelia.
Soy todo lo que soy gracias a ti.

Contents

Acknowledgments   xi

1. Research Grief   1
2. Abuelita Theology   19
3. A Sabiduría That Heals   38
4. Mujeres of Exodus   51
5. Telling La Verdad   66
6. Cosiendo and Creating   81
7. Sobreviviendo   95
8. Protesta and Persistence   116
9. Desesperación   130
10. A Divine Baile   146
11. Madre of Exile   159
12. Resolviendo in La Lucha   173

Notes   191
Bibliography   200

Acknowledgments

How do I even begin to thank or acknowledge the myriad of people who have floated in and out of my life, who have played decisive roles in the construction of this work even before it was written? I owe this book to a cloud of mujeres (women), ancestors, witnesses, and saints in my past who have paved the way, believing in the liberative love of God and acting in response to that belief.

To the women in my life who formed me from childhood, had faith in me, cared for me: Mom—your unrelenting support has carried me through every moment of my life. Thank you for always believing in me and loving me the best way you could. Ash—your unwavering love has shaped me. Mama and Lela—my childhood would have been incomplete without your care for me. Yetz—your consistent presence grounds me. Amanda—your depth and encouragement has changed me. This work is one about each and every one of us making meaning of life, God, and our existence. I thank you all for playing a pivotal role.

Thank you to other mujeres who have inspired me, have listened to my vision and dream from its inception, and have offered encouragement along the way: Nicole—I literally couldn't have done this without you. Esther—you're my rock. Biankha—you've always believed in me. Thank you to Ana Estevez, Naty Espinales, Gaby Perez-Julio de Zamora, Natasha Santana, Karen González, Jenn Guerra Aldana, Roslyn Hernandez, Inés Velázquez Mc-Bryde, Teesha Hadra, Bethany Banks, Lacey Lanier, Sandy Ovalle, Melody Jalandoon, Sandra Van Opstal, Shelley and Liz Cole, Haley Johnston, Elizabeth Staszak, Irene Cho, my Nodie crew, my agent, Rachelle Gardner, and the incredible Brazos team. Each of you has brought this process to life—whether directly or indirectly, in the past or in the present.

To the men in my life who have supported me, elevated my voice, trusted the Holy Spirit's work in me, and treated me with love, dignity, and respect: thank you. I am who I am because of you. Especially you, Taylor—you are my home, my safe space, my sounding board. This book would be nothing without you.

A special shout-out to my animal kin in the past and present, who have reminded me that this world and all its life and creatures are interconnected: Muka, Sasha, Max, Scully, and Mulder.

Lastly, to Abuela Evelia, Abuela Flora, and the Cuban soil that birthed them—I am forever indebted to your wisdom and your love.

1

Research Grief

I sat in bed staring at my laptop, the dozens of Google tabs detailing the journey I'd been on. Books were buried in my comforter, creating a type of literary war zone. My ojeras (the bags under my eyes) decorated my face the color of day-old bruises. I kept opening the folder on my phone titled "Do Not Open," robotically scrolling through each social media app to distract myself from the sharp, sucker-punch pain in my gut that had lingered for days. It wasn't the first time I had felt the pangs that come when the past reveals itself to you, when an unknown history digs itself up from the grave. Colonizer or colonized, oppressor or oppressed—there's a moment after the deep, dark, often lonely work of becoming our own archaeologists that the pangs hit. It's a surprising pain that often comes when we dig up the skeletons from the ground, when we realize the dirt we stand on is tainted and the reality we've been fed is curated.

While this wasn't the first time reality hit, it would be the first time it pulled a fast one on me while I was writing an academic paper—a process, I was told, that was supposed to be "objective," a discipline solely of the mind. Up until this point, no one had warned me this would happen, that the work would feel this personal. The dominating culture taught me to separate myself from what I study, and consequently, to live with a fragmented identity. But when our musings about life and faith exist only in fragments, we live disembodied realities. God becomes disembodied too.

It's easier when we're fed what to think, what to believe about ourselves, our histories, and God. When our identities are programmed, we're not taught to really engage or to bring our whole selves to the table. We're taught our own thoughts and hearts cannot be trusted in any way, and thus we live in shame, a widened chasm. But something painful and terribly beautiful happens when that chasm begins to narrow. I think this narrowing, this shrinking space where theology, history, and our identities—hearts, minds, bodies, and souls—begin to blend together, is where the pangs are felt most sharply.

It may not feel like it in the moment, but this is also part of the journey toward liberation.

That day while in bed with my laptop and books open, that chasm narrowed again. Reality paid a painful visit. And it didn't come alone. It brought grief along with it—that deep, gut-wrenching sense of grief. It was a sorrow from a time deep in the past, before I even existed—a grief that my antepasados, my ancestors, knew, one that hovered above time, spanning history.

What do you do with generational grief?

I sat in it for a while. And then I got to work.

Initially I called the angst that I felt that day "research grief"; it's the grief that comes when getting deep into the thick of researching difficult topics. Surprisingly, this is a common thing in the academic world. I once heard of a woman who began losing sleep, her hair, and her sanity during her time as a doctoral student writing her dissertation on the Holocaust. Even trying to make sense of other people's trauma can traumatize.

This notable pang of research grief surfaced early in my seminary career during a Women in Church History and Theology class. Though I was several courses into my master of divinity program, I was new to exploring the topics of women and people of color as they pertain to theology. The dominating culture had yet to invite me to see myself and my culture within God's story.

But I thank Creator for my stubbornness, for my combative spirit, which the dominating culture has deemed too much— muy fresca.

When I began this course, I was attending my second seminary. I had left the first one only months prior, after tussling with professors and pastors and experiencing firsthand the demons of sexism and racism. I admit, being raised in an immigrant Roman Catholic community and then transitioning to Protestantism as an adult left me unfamiliar with the ins and outs of evangelicalism. Not only was I blissfully ignorant of what I was stepping into spiritually, but as a Cuban American born and raised in a city predominantly made up of Cuban Americans, I had yet to wrestle with my cultural identity in a majority, non-Hispanic white context.

———

I was sitting in my hermeneutics class at the first seminary I attended when I realized I needed to leave—it was a difficult day. As the professor taught us how to engage interpretation week after week, it became clear that he wasn't speaking to me. The lens from which he taught and from which he encouraged us to engage was his own, of course. He was born and raised on a small farm in the rural South, so the context from which he understood the world was such, and the way he taught us to engage Scripture reflected this reality too. I remember constantly feeling like nothing he taught about the world, life, or the Bible related to me. I grew up in a large Latine[1] city where I danced salsa on the weekends and greeted strangers with a kiss on the cheek. I was conceived and born out of wedlock, and I lived the first part of my life in a small apartment with my single mother in La Sagüesera, the southwest portion of Miami, where I owned my first fake ID at sixteen. These details made me feel tainted, like I didn't belong. Was I not domesticated or pure enough? Did the reality of my life, experiences, and worldview make me too much or position me too far from understanding and knowing God the way I was supposed to? Trying to learn how to do the work of interpretation within a rural Southern framework only made me feel further from God—and made me feel like my experiences, community, and culture were only getting in the way of my being able to understand the Bible. As a newer evangelical, I was told that shame was no longer mine to bear, but how could I not feel shame as a Latine woman trying to fit the mold of whiteness?

Activist Julia Serano once said, "A woman of color doesn't face racism and sexism separately; the sexism she faces is often racialized, and the racism she faces is often sexualized."[2] This truth began to feel personal to me. One day this same professor went off on a tangent about how important it is for everyone to learn Greek and Hebrew, as it changes the way we read and teach Scripture. It seemed to me that he really was speaking only to the men in the class when he finished his speech with, "And ladies, your husbands will be really impressed if you can exegete Scripture alongside them." My heart sank; I was stunned that he would imply I was going through the effort of learning the biblical languages simply to impress my spouse. I nearly fell off my chair when he ended by asking, "Right, Kat?" I was one of the outspoken students in class. The mujeres, the women, in my culture taught me to be that way—to be confident, to speak up, to work hard. I carried this with me in seminary. Not only did I debate theology, exegete Scripture, and have an educated opinion alongside my male peers, but I also spent just as much of my personal time studying as they did—and according to my professor, it was not to eventually lead the church but to impress my spouse.

At this point I had already begun my in-depth study of women in Scripture. I had already learned about the household codes, women leaders in the Bible, the context from which Paul spoke, and a myriad of other details that convinced me that God had uniquely called me and empowered me to lead, to use my gifts and my talents, and to do so from the strength of my abuela (my grandmother), my mom, and the cloud of antepasadas before them.

Through my study of Scripture, I had learned that God didn't make a mistake in creating me a woman, and God surely didn't make a mistake in creating me a Cuban woman. The shame that I felt for not fitting the mold of whiteness and patriarchy soon began to lift, and I was able to see the ways that the divine met me in the midst of my complex, multilayered identity, background, and experiences. I admit, this is an ongoing journey.

After class that day, I arrived at home still in a state of disbelief and pain, feeling as if my hard work, my calling, my dignity had been ripped from me. I walked through the door, looked at my brand-new spouse only weeks after our wedding, and muttered, "I think we need to get out of here."

"OK," he said. "Where should we go?"

A week later, while I was still at that same seminary, another professor taught about how different Bible translations altered the paragraph formations in Ephesians 5, which affects how we read it and thus how we translate it. In some translations, a new paragraph begins with verse 22 (and oftentimes with its own heading), signaling that submission belongs primarily to wives. But the original Greek doesn't have headings or verse numbers. So this command, my professor taught us, is supposed to flow from the verse before it, which teaches about mutual submission. Realizing what he may have been trying to imply, I nearly jumped out of my seat.

After class, I confessed to the professor that I was thinking of transferring to a different seminary. He encouraged me to go, reminding me of the potential I had and the little opportunity there was for me to grow in a context that doesn't affirm women in all aspects of ministry.

A few weeks later my spouse and I had our entire lives packed inside my Kia. But at that moment, I didn't know where we'd end up, just like I didn't know where the decolonizing journey would take me: to a new state, a new city, and a new seminary, where I would study the history of my isla, my island, and how it intersects with my faith. I also didn't know how much more I would learn, what I would reject or embrace. It was a scary and uncertain space, but a sacred one nonetheless. I realize now how dangerous it is to think we've arrived at enlightenment, at certainty, about ourselves, about God. I'm still figuring it all out day by day. Some days I'm confident and hopeful. And others? Well, other days I just get by.

There was one thing I did know for certain that day I learned about Ephesians 5. I learned that God really does work in mysterious ways and places—and through unexpected people. This detail alone makes the journey exhilarating.

It wasn't until I made that first painful exodus that I felt the freedom to begin inviting every aspect of who I am into my study and work as a theologian. It was in the second seminary, in that Women in Church History and Theology class, I was encouraged to explore how my past has shaped my present, and it proved to be another turning point in my life and ministry.

After ten weeks of diving deep into the lives of overlooked women in Christianity's past—women like Perpetua, Felicitas, Julian of Norwich, and Katharina Schütz Zell—I began to see how their work, though often unrecognized, changed history. I know we wouldn't be where we are today if it wasn't for the sacrifice of these women who dreamed about God and wrote about God and were often silenced, labeled heretics, or worse, simply ignored because they did so. However, this discovery left me hungry to learn more. What about las mujeres, the women whose lives directly influenced mine? The border crossers, those who inhabited multiple in-between worlds?

As a daughter of immigrants who was raised in a city of immigrants, I always had a deep connection to mi isla, my island, Cuba. However, before this time, my antepasadas—the women whose shoulders I now stand on, whose experiences live inside my body, and whose sacrifices paved the way for my present reality—had never been a part of the theological narrative in any "formal" sense.

When beginning my research, I didn't know how far the rabbit trail of digging into the history of mi gente, my people, would take me. While I knew our past was painful, I was naive and eager to take on the task of learning more about it. Back at home, we didn't talk too much about our history. Sure, we were—are—proud and unapologetically Cuban, but because the details of my family's past are tender and complicated, they are oftentimes uncomfortable to talk about. There was so much I wanted to learn, however, so I looked forward to understanding the way Christianity intersects with the country that birthed my abuelita[3] and my mother—the two strong and courageous women who raised me.

The first book I picked up was Miguel De La Torre's *The Quest for the Cuban Christ*. I left the library that day looking forward to reading about Jesus and my foremothers and forefathers. But needless to say, my excitement quickly dissipated when I read the first page: "Women were raped. Children were disemboweled. Men fell prey to the invaders' swords."[4]

I immediately knew this journey would be dark, heavy, and difficult. And the worst part? This was only the beginning of the written history of my people. This information would redirect the course of my ministry and how I understood theology, who I am, and the ways the two intersect.

The story of mi gente involves the story of the native Cubans—the Taínos—being invaded and tortured by Spain. Worse, it tells how Spain would use their imported "Christ" to justify the greed for gold and glory.[5] Spain would exploit and oppress the so-called heathens they encountered in the name of this imported "Christ," who would support the ethnocide and genocide of the Taínos as well as the forced transportation of hundreds of thousands of enslaved African people to the island.[6] And as we know, ethnocide, genocide, slavery, and forced relocation aren't isolated to Cuban history but describe the history of Native people across the globe.

Many people generally know that the Jesus they've been singing about and singing to—and the beloved symbol of his cross—has historically been used as a weapon of hate, pain, and oppression, but something changes when a person first realizes how deep the colonial wounds truly run. This shift is colossal. Disorienting. What do you do with this information? Many throw in the towel and abandon the whole thing—understandably. The feelings of betrayal can be overwhelming. Others go through seasons of lament, grief, anger. This process has often been called "deconstruction" or a "decolonizing" of the faith—the unlinking of ourselves from a god we thought we knew, from a colonial Christianity, from an imported and imperial Christ. While uncomfortable, the journey from one place of knowledge, one way of being and knowing, to another way of understanding and seeing the world is crucial and even sacred.

Gloria Anzaldúa calls this space "nepantla." Nepantla is the Náhuatl (an Indigenous group of people from Mexico and Central America) word for an in-between state, un espacio entre medio. The nepantla is the uncertain terrain that we cross when changing from one place to another. It is a space of constant tension where transformation and healing may be possible.[7] Our journeys of decolonizing and indigenizing, of deconstruction and reconstruction are that of nepantla. They are sacred spaces of learning, growing, shifting, becoming.

My nepantla journey didn't begin that day sitting on my bed with my tabs open and my ojeras bright purple. But that day was when I became aware that I was on it. In fact, thinking back, that day stands out as another turning point on this journey. I'm reminded of Rachel's husband, Jacob, who built a sacred stone pillar in Luz, "to the God who answered me when I was in trouble and who has been with me wherever I've gone" (Gen. 35:3).

That day and the day in my hermeneutics class serve as stones of remembrance on my life's altar—reminders that the divine has been with me wherever I've gone.

On that day, while reading De La Torre, I became curious to know more about the Christian European invaders—the representatives of Christ, who claimed allegiance to the "true" God of the Bible while ignoring the Bible's basic call for justice.[8] I became curious about the Christ they claimed too. I wondered, Can this Christ—the one who has infiltrated much of our theology and mission efforts—the Christ who is white, elite, and of European descent, be redeemed? Is this the Jesus who "saved" me?

Or could there be another Christ? The one whom many of us have been in search of, the one of los humildes, the humble, as De La Torre calls them? My journey began to be shaped by the desire to learn about Jesus from the perspective of los humildes—the colonized, the marginalized, those who didn't get to write the history and theology books. In many ways, they are the ones intimately acquainted with the Jesus of the Gospels—the bicultural, border-crossing, Brown Jesus, the one born in a stable, rejected in his hometown, tortured, broken, and battered. I knew that in order to understand this Jesus better, I would have to prioritize listening to and centering the voices of los humildes.

I kept reading. "Upon the female body are found the scars of colonialism and domination."[9] Throughout history, Black, Indigenous, and other women of color have borne the brunt of colonization through slavery, subjugation, and sexual exploitation. These colonial and patriarchal wounds still linger today. As a result, poor and marginalized women are among the most underrepresented in our society, their voices often ignored. As I reflected on this, I realized that the more time I spend around women the world overlooks, women who bear the scars of colonization, the more I recognize that they understand something the rest of us don't. Their remarkably intimate relationship with the Brown Jesus of los humildes is the kind of connection many of us with differing levels of privilege long for. I didn't have to search too far to find these women; I was raised, shaped, and formed by them.

But why are their theological insights overlooked, and why are they never invited to share their wisdom? In my experience, our spiritual ancestors, our madres (mothers) of the faith, were always the objects of narratives, the ones talked about but never talking themselves. The more I wrestled with this, the more I wondered, *In our fight for liberation, are we seeking to ensure that overlooked and unrecognized peoples act as protagonists of their own stories?* Too often, women—particularly marginalized women—are the heroines of someone else's story, or worse yet, someone else (usually a man) is the hero of theirs. This wrestling is where I received the inspiration for this book as well as a podcast. My quest to find protagonistas (protagonists) initially led me to buy a microphone, download editing software, and begin sending emails to Black, Indigenous, and other women of color in my networks. A few months later my podcast, *The Protagonistas*, was birthed into the world.

What made this process so meaningful was not just that I got to speak and learn from protagonistas in my networks but that with each conversation, I reflected on the most personal and significant protagonista in my own life. You see, even after several years of formal seminary education, I can honestly say that the most impactful, albeit unrecognized, theologian in my life is a woman of valor who modeled wisdom, strength, survival, persistence, and resistance—a woman just like the one praised in Proverbs 31:

> A woman whose value exceeds pearls,
> whose husband[s] entrusted their heart[s] to her,
> who ran businesses,
> provided food for all in the familia,
> planted fruit from her gardens,
> who gave to the needy,
> who [literally] made her own garments and sold them,
> who wore strength and honor as her clothing,
> who was confident about the future,
> whose mouth was full of wisdom,
> whose children bless her
> whose husband[s] praised her.
>
> —the *eshet chayil* of Proverbs 31
> (vv. 10–31, my translation)

My abuelita.

The beautiful thing is that my abuelita is one of the millions of abuelitas—as well as tías (aunts) and madres—who have formed us and our beliefs. Many of us have or know a strong, devoted, unrecognized theologian who has served as a madre of our faith, a beacon of light on our spiritual journey, whether she is biologically related or not. This book is an invitation not only to celebrate these women but to consider them genuine sources of theology.

Throughout these pages, you will be met with stories of la lucha, the struggle, for liberation. Black, Indigenous, and other women of color are deeply acquainted with the depths of this struggle.

This book explores an abuelita faith through the lenses of my abuela and other unnamed and overlooked madrinas (godmothers) of the faith in Scripture and beyond. It is an attempt to tell a familiar story of displacement and belonging. Within these pages are stories of raw, grassroots faith and its close friend, survival. While these stories are unique, they aren't unusual. Many are remarkably familiar among many marginalized women—from before the time of Jesus through our current day. Part of what makes their stories so familiar is that, historically, they've remained untold. But I often wonder, What if by silencing these women, we've missed something profound? *What if the world's greatest theologians are those whom the world wouldn't consider theologians at all?*

I love the Bible—I find its stories fascinating. I love to study it and talk about it for many reasons, but one of the main reasons is that, frankly, it's not going anywhere. As some have pointed out, the Bible doesn't just reflect history; it makes it.[10] The Bible isn't just a book about the past; it affects the way present-day decisions are made. For centuries Scripture has been used and misused to justify atrocities across the globe, and as a Western, biblically educated Christian, my conviction is to offer tools so that others can read and reread it through life-giving lenses, as I believe liberation is central to God's story.

Although the Bible has been used as a weapon of destruction in many ways, it's also important to acknowledge that throughout the centuries, marginalized people have found themselves within the narrative too—often claiming the Bible's "reality" as their own and thus exceeding the bounds of imperial exegesis.[11]

For example, Rigoberta Menchú is a Quiché Mayan organizer and activist who led her community in standing against the Guatemalan government, which was seeking to exterminate her people. From reading the Bible, Menchú learned that it is her people's—and other oppressed people's—right to defend themselves against oppressive and colonialist powers. "For us the Bible is our main weapon. It has shown us the way," she says.

> Perhaps those who call themselves Christians, but who are really only Christians in theory, won't understand why we give the Bible the meaning we do. But that's because they haven't lived as we have. And also perhaps because they can't analyze it. I can assure that any one of my community, even though he's illiterate and has to have it read to him and translated into his language, can learn many lessons from it, because he has no difficulty understanding what reality is and what the difference is between the paradise above, in Heaven, and the reality of our people here on Earth.[12]

Menchú's activism—her fight for her Indigenous community against colonial exploitation (for which she was awarded a Nobel Peace Prize)—was born from her personal study of Scripture. While the Bible has been weaponized by oppressors, it has also served as a beacon of hope and strength by the oppressed. My hope is to highlight the latter within these pages.

As you read, you may notice that I ask more questions than give answers when it comes to Scripture. For me, questions are an invitation to stay curious and to keep listening. Oftentimes, when we feel like we have the answers, we stop paying attention—and I never want to stop listening or paying attention to the divine voice within the pages of the Bible. I also hope that, with my questions, I can give our theological imaginations an opportunity to soar, to see the text with new eyes, and to find fresh insights. To this end, my exegesis is not exhaustive. Instead, I offer alternative readings that are in no way objective or universal.

<hr/>

Throughout these pages I also highlight the ways that my abuelita's faith has affected my own. It follows how I came to learn, unlearn, and relearn much of how I read the Bible and understand God.

Before I get into this, however, it's important to state my social location and position. My intention is to be inclusive, but I don't speak for all Latine people or women. Despite the dominating culture's attempt to stick us into one category—"Hispanic" or even "Latino/a"—our cultures and experiences are layered, diverse, and unique. I am a second-generation Cuban American born and raised in the Cuban community of Miami, Florida— these are important details that shape me and speak into the context of this book. Being a second-generation Latina means that my perspectives are different than first- or even third-generation peoples. Additionally, the fact that I'm a US-based Latina means that my experiences and understandings of the world are different than Latine peoples who live in Latin America.

Being raised in a city where my culture is the dominant culture also influences my reality. I don't know if you've ever been to Miami—strolled down Calle Ocho (Eighth Street) to watch all the old Cuban men play dominoes and smoke Cuban cigars— but it's a remarkable place, unlike any other. Many have referred to it as the capital of Latin America in the US, where strangers go in for a kiss on the cheek, Spanglish—a mixture between English and Spanish—is the primary language spoken, and Cuban restaurants populate every street corner.

Miami's Cuban population made national headlines in the 2020 presidential election for its pro-Trump affinities, making it an interesting case study for what it means to be Latine and how we, as a people, are to wrestle with our collective—and individual—identity. While many non-Hispanic white, (mostly) liberal commentators were perplexed by how many people in our community voted, many Latines I know were not surprised.

Similarly, I saw news headline after news headline referencing "the Latino vote," as if our community weren't marked by a myriad of countries with their own histories, backgrounds, and cultural customs that influence each of us uniquely. The political opinions and overall experiences of the Latine community are diverse. If the dominating culture has learned anything about us, I hope it's that we are not a monolith. Like many other Latine peoples, my city and mi gente in particular hold a multilayered identity born out of a complicated history that bear the scars of colonial wounds.

⸻

While most Cuban American history focuses on post-Castro immigration, it's important to note that many Cubans arrived in the US as early as the nineteenth century. This early group was composed primarily of Afro-Cubans who established themselves in different parts of Florida, including Tampa and Key West.[13] Nearly a century later, just after the 1959 revolution, another large wave of Cubans arrived in the US. During this time over 150,000 refugees landed in Miami, most of them white, elite, professional, and educated. Although they still faced ethnic discrimination in housing and employment (it was common to find signs in Miami that read "No Cubans, no pets, no children" and "Dade County is not Cuba, speak English!"), they were able to use their connections, wealth, and time to build roots and reestablish themselves in ways similar to their past.[14] Another wave happened shortly after and lasted through the early 1970s, bringing nearly three hundred thousand refugees, most of whom were semiskilled working-class people, and many of whom designated themselves as "other race" or mixed.[15] A majority of this group was also women, children, and seniors.

My abuelo, grandfather, came to this country during the second wave of immigrants. What I think makes his story so unique is that he was among the balseros (boat people)—a less honorable term for those who arrived in the US not by plane but on a raft. I've always found it interesting that to many within the dominant culture, those who leave their country for a chance at a better life are often frowned on, thought of as less than, without honor.

It's curious because I cannot think of anything more honorable than doing whatever you can or have to do in order to provide a better life for your family.

Yet another wave of Cuban immigrants arrived in Miami in the 1980s after thousands of Cubans on the island were able to storm through the gates of the Peruvian embassy, seeking asylum primarily from the poor economic situation on the island. After Castro opened the port of Mariel, over 125,000 refugees crossed the Florida Straits; a majority of these were young Afro-Cubans.

With time, Miami became a haven, a place where Cubans were able re-create their past and grasp firmly to the memory of their isla.

De La Torre uses the term *Ajiaco*—a Cuban stew consisting of different meats, indigenous roots, and tropical vegetables—to describe who Cubans are and the formation of their diverse ethnic backgrounds. From the Amerindians we have maíz (corn), papa (potato), malanga (taro), boniato (sweet potato), and others. The Spaniards included calabaza (pumpkin) and nabo (turnip). Chinese peoples added a myriad of spices, and Africans contributed ñame (yams) and more. This mestizaje (mixture) of flavors, races, and cultures offers a stew of identities that come together on the stove of the Caribbean.[16]

In the same way, Miami became what it is not only because of the mass exodus of Cubans who fled their island after Fidel Castro took power but because of the mix of Nicaraguan, Haitian, Honduran, Dominican, Colombian, Jamaican, and other cultures that contribute to its collective "Ajiaco stew."

The notion of a multiflavored stew with a variety of ingredients simmering together can also symbolize what it means to be a Latine person. While this mixture of cultures and races contributes to our rich diversity, it also adds complexity to how this diversity is lived out. Historically, it has resulted in the silencing of the Black and Indigenous cultures and voices that make up the Cuban and broader Latine community. The hope, the goal, is that each flavor plays a unique role in the creation of the final masterpiece—not that one flavor be elevated at the expense of another.

As I mentioned, my lens is that of a second-generation Cuban American who has swum Westernized waters her entire life. What's unique about the second-generation experience is the complexity to being Westernized and US American while simultaneously having nondominant ways of communicating and understanding the world. Leaving Miami made me realize how different my childhood was compared to that of many of my non-Hispanic white friends. Being from a city made up of immigrants who have been displaced from their country offers its own particular lens. I've swum in waters that are traumatized, are shaped by exile and displacement, and in many ways, look to the empire, to the United States, as a sort of salvation. But that's what empire does, doesn't it? It puts people in vulnerable positions and then convinces them that only the empire can save them from their vulnerability.

My decolonizing efforts seek to name that complexity.

Because of Cubans' prevailing presence and success in Miami, I've also swum in waters that carry varying levels of privilege. I took one of my final seminary courses with the Hispanic Summer Program, an ecumenical enrichment program for Latine students. During one of our first sessions, our professor asked us to share experiences we had with our ethnicity growing up. One by one, each classmate—most of whom had arrived in the States to study as international students from Latin America—began to share that the notion of being a minority person was new to them. They hadn't thought about it prior to moving and were surprised when they suddenly became "people of color" overnight. Although I had been born in the US, I felt a sense of solidarity with my classmates, as my experience of leaving Miami felt similar. De La Torre also grew up in Miami and moved to the South as an adult. He articulates my experience exactly: he states that he went to bed one night as a white person in Miami and woke up the next morning as a Brown person in the South.[17]

These realities—the disadvantages I experience from being part of a "minority group" in the dominant culture's eyes as well as the advantages I experience because of my skin color, documentation status, and level of education—all add to the complexities of who I am: the multiple identities that I hold and from which I understand and navigate the world.

In Miami, the longing for Cuba has become "the unifying substance of the Exilic Cuban's existential being," representing a common past, symbolically linking us to the land we left behind.[18] Mi gente are a people perpetually in exile, and like the Israelites did, Cubans dream of the promised land. But their promised land lives only in their memories. Much of this longing from my familia and the community around me has been passed down from generation to generation.

It's an odd thing to feel nostalgia for a land you've never lived on, but if we've learned anything from our ancestors in Scripture and beyond: the land lives within us. My soul remembers the familiar rhythms of my island, and I can feel the congas and my heart beating as one.

2

Abuelita Theology

When I've talked about abuelita theology in the past, many have asked, quite simply, What is it? A fair question, but one that is difficult to answer because abuelita theology is deeply personal. For me, it is created in real time as I decolonize: decenter and recenter, deconstruct and reconstruct.

It is the practice of uncovering and naming our abuelas who have inspired, taught, and guided us in our process of becoming and belonging. In this sense, I like to think of not *one* abuelita theology but *multiple* abuelita theologies born from the diversity that makes up the lived experiences of marginalized women across religious expressions, races, ethnicities, cultures, classes, and places. Developing or articulating this theology won't have a linear, Western, or modern definition. Instead, we must not only stop to listen but pause to reflect: Where, when, and how have we been ministered to or mothered by abuelitas—those in the present and those who came before us?

While this chapter might feel a little academic, this isn't an academic book. An academic book may come, but introducing an abuelita theology first through personal and biblical narrative told through the everyday lives of women, is important for me because that's the essence of abuelita theology. It's a theology birthed through lo cotidiano, the everyday. It is not lofty but informal. Some call abuelita theology "kitchen theology" because it is formed in the kitchen—while the frijoles negros (black beans) are simmering on the stove, the floor is being mopped, and the cafecito (coffee) is brewing. Abuelita theology takes form while family members are sitting around la mesa (the table) discussing la lucha, the struggle of everyday life. Thus, this book is an invitation into la sala (the living room) of my experiences and my perspectives from growing up as a daughter of Cuban immigrants.

Now, I wish to be honest when talking about abuelita theology. While I seek to honor and elevate the voices of our grandmothers and "abuelita theologians" through Scripture, I also want to be careful to not romanticize or essentialize their lives or experiences. Their stories and reflections hold both beauty and pain. Many people I know still carry wounds from ideologies perpetuated by their abuelitas, whether they be from gender or patriarchal stereotypes, body shaming, anti-Blackness, or strict cultural norms—our abuelitas inhabit a complex reality. In the same way, abuelita theology as a kitchen theology reflects the beautifully communal and natural formation of faith in la cocina, the kitchen. However, this reality is true primarily because our abuelitas are often relegated to la cocina due to the existence of machismo. Thus, abuelita theology inhabits a complicated, interstitial[1] space, as we will see.

Your journey and mine are shaped by a collective cultural memory. Theologian Jeanette Rodriguez explains that culture has been the means of human survival. Human cultures have survived many threats by interpreting, adapting, and resisting dominant cultures that are more "powerful." This is done primarily through our capacity to remember, create, and re-create our past. *Cultural memory*, then, refers to a collective knowledge from one generation to the next that gives many of us a chance to reconstruct our cultural identity. It is characterized by the survival of a historically, politically, and socially marginalized people and by the role of spirituality as a form of resistance. For Rodriguez, "cultural memory is about making meaningful statements about the past in a given cultural context of the present conditions."[2]

This, too, is the essence of abuelita faith: it requires that I dive into the treasure chest of the collective, cultural memory of those who came before me. As you read the chapters of this book and reflect on my story alongside the stories of women in the Bible, I encourage you also to dive in. We are shaped by the memory of our antepasados, our ancestors, the cloud of witnesses who went before us.

I also seek to articulate an abuelita faith through decolonized and postcolonial lenses. The term *postcolonial* was created to give voice to the most vulnerable and poorest members of the global community. Postcolonialism deals with colonization or colonized peoples, focusing on the way in which literature by the colonizing culture distorts the experiences and realities of colonized peoples as well as assumes their inferiority. It seeks to reclaim the identity of colonized people who were shaped by the idea of *otherness*.[3]

The idea of the other, which was perpetuated by European colonizers, has been used as a way for those in power to maintain authority over those they are colonizing. An imperialist sees the other as different from the self in order to commodify control over the other's identity. The self and the other are the colonizer and the colonized, respectively, or the familiar and the foreign— the one who does not belong to the group, who doesn't speak a given language, or who doesn't have the same customs.[4]

Dominating culture has othered many of our abuelitas because of the language or dialect they speak, their accent, the pigmentation of their skin, their cultural customs, their lack of Western education, their socioeconomic status, and/or their gender. The concept of otherness sees the world as divided into mutually excluding opposites. While the self (the colonizer) is ordered, rational, masculine, and good, the other (the colonized) is chaotic, irrational, feminine, and evil. The current dominating culture may not say this with its words, but what is presented as "normal" or "common" perpetuates this myth.

Throughout history the colonizer has been the one to "know" and "theorize," while the colonized can only be known or theorized about. Therefore, postcolonialism advocates thinking *with* the marginalized rather than thinking *about* them. My hope is that when we engage with colonized, grassroots, or overlooked persons, whether in society or in Scripture, we listen not to consume, to take, or to appropriate but to hold sacred space, to learn, and to make room for the holy, where God is often at work in lo cotidiano, the informal space where life and faith happen, where a myriad of decisions are made—decisions that many of us with varying levels of privilege never even have to consider.

As I've read the narratives of many marginalized women in Scripture, I've sought to notice not only the countless decisions they make for their familias but what these decisions communicate. What is in the details? What is left unsaid? What can we draw from the voice of the other in Scripture, the one whom God so deeply cares about and seeks to protect and honor? My hope is that the stories of these overlooked and unnamed women will give us a chance to listen to "them" talking to "us"—instead of "us" talking about or to "them."[5] I also hope that when we uncover and listen to their often silenced voices, we will tune our ears to those same voices in our midst. As we imagine these narratives in Scripture, may we reread these texts with eyes to see the abuelas who have grandmothered and mothered us, not just our own biological abuelas but our madrinas and co-madres both in the present and in the past. My hope is that we recognize how much more we have to learn—not from books but from lived experiences—and that these experiences may help us change the way we see the world and those who have something valuable to offer us.

For me, abuelita theology is about looking into the real, raw outworking of faith.

Before we can hear and recognize these voices in Scripture, however, we must first understand that the lens through which many have read and been trained to understand the Bible has predominantly been a Western, male, European lens. These voices have dominated our pulpits and our commentaries, the places from which many of us have been educated, trained, or spiritually formed. This has left the insight, interpretations, and perspectives of Black, Latine, Asian, and Indigenous writers as secondary.

In 2019, John MacArthur, a prominent evangelical pastor, appeared in a widely shared video not only telling Bible study teacher Beth Moore to "go home" but also criticizing Southern Baptist Convention (SBC) leaders for their suggestion that there should never be another Bible translation committee without a Latine, Black, or woman scholar on it. MacArthur scoffed at the suggestion and responded by questioning, "Translation of the Bible? How about someone who knows Greek and Hebrew?"[6] The SBC has a clear history of racism, but surely they weren't implying that knowledge of the biblical languages is unnecessary for translation committees. And surely MacArthur knows this (or perhaps he doesn't?). His apparent disregard for the lived experiences and cultural insights of those who are unlike him perpetuates ideology that excludes the majority of the world from the theological table.

Because of this, I like to think that this work, my work, as a Latina theologian, writer, and emerging biblical scholar is an act of dissent. As others have said before, *my existence is resistance.*

First, any attempt I make to present a theology that is decentered from the dominant narrative and recentered to focus on or highlight the perspectives of marginalized women will inevitably be filtered through a Western lens, because I am a Western individual. I am on the same journey of decolonization as you might be.

Second, as Latino scholar Oscar García-Johnson illuminated for me, any attempt to incorporate decolonized thinking, particularly in the context of US American culture, will necessarily feed into a colonial narrative. The crux of colonial thinking is embedded in perceived binary dichotomies—and no matter how hard I try to come away from these colonial binaries, my work will be put in some sort of category: liberal or conservative, left or right. This is true especially as someone from the Cuban American community. Many Cubans in the US who were affected by the revolution hold strict political stances—understandably. On the one hand, if I—or anyone else in my community—is critical of any of the positions they might hold, we might quickly be labeled a "socialist" in a derogatory way. On the other hand, being sympathetic to the trauma of exile and displacement might cause many progressives to question if I am no longer on their side.

The human experience—our stories as well as those of our abuelitas—are often more nuanced and complicated than the boxes set before us, the ones we've been forced to fit into. Although I do so imperfectly, I try to hold these complexities with care.

I often wonder if the strict colonial binaries set before us are what have hurt so many people within the church. For so long church leaders have told us that we are loved no matter what, while simultaneously telling us that if we don't hold to a specific way of understanding God, a certain category of belief, we are at risk of damnation. The first time I was called a heretic was for believing that women could preach, a belief based on my in-depth study of the biblical text. I wasn't called a heretic because I denied the Trinity, the resurrection, or any of the core tenets of Christianity.

Perhaps so many young Christians are fleeing from the church because of these dichotomous, "all or nothing" views of faith that disregard life's complexities—the views of faith that gloss over the messiness of life mirrored by the biblical characters and stories that we hold so dear. As the rest of this book will show, Scripture is a beautiful and nuanced account of the chaos of life and faith.

To construct decolonized thinking, we must set aside dichoto-mies that stereotype and force people into boxes—in order to recover the voices of the underrepresented, the marginalized voices that get lost in the middle.

Now I want to be clear: I'm not saying that there isn't right or wrong. Injustice, dehumanization, and oppression of people are always wrong. When the image of God is violated, destroyed, dishonored, or unprotected, that is wrong, "an act of violence," as Black author Osheta Moore points out.[7] Instead, nonbinary language resists the notion of reducing people—particularly mar-ginalized people—to objects that can be easily categorized and understood.

Before describing the details of abuelita faith (as I understand it) already articulated by a few scholars, including Virgilio Eli-zondo, Loida Martell-Otero, Miguel De La Torre, and Robert Chao Romero, I want to introduce other theological frameworks that have marked this journey. Besides the studies of decoloniza-tion and postcolonialism, these include (but are not limited to) womanist biblical hermeneutics, mujerista theology, feminist intercultural theology, and Latina evangélica thought. Each of these have helped shape my understanding of theology from the perspective of los humildes.

Womanist biblical hermeneutics. Womanist scholar Mitzi Smith notes that womanist biblical hermeneutics prioritize the communal and particular lived experiences and histories of Black women and other women of color as not only a central point but a starting point, as well as a general interpretative lens for critical analysis of the Bible, contexts, cultures, readers, and readings. "Womanists sing, write, and speak from the margins for the margins—the doubly marginalized, the black woman called to preach in the black church, the single black mother, the motherless black child, the pregnant unwed mother striving to find a home in the black church. We testify that the God in us is great, compassionate, courageous, audacious, loving, nonjudgmental, and empowering."[8] Womanist biblical hermeneutics has helped me to engage with this God in Scripture, in myself, and in the world.

Mujerista theology and feminist intercultural theology. Fellow Cuban Ada Maria Isasi-Díaz coined the term *mujerista theology*, which is liberation theology from a Latina perspective. Liberation theology originated as a prophetic movement responding to human suffering—more specifically, poverty and injustice in the popular sectors of Latin America. It highlights the social concerns of poor and oppressed people, as Jesus emphasized in much of his ministry. Liberation theology has taught me that theology cannot be divorced from personal story. Story is what connects theory with reality, what gives life to our religious understandings.

In this vein, mujerista theology takes the narratives and lived experiences of women seriously, emphasizing the unique struggle of Latinas at the intersection of ethnicity, race, gender, and socioeconomic status. Isasi-Díaz began developing this theology after her time serving as a missionary to Peru. There, she realized not only that liberation is necessary for justice and peace but that one cannot be liberated at the expense of another or isolated from others.[9] Thus, mujerista theology is a process of empowerment for marginalized women that begins with the development of a strong sense of moral agency. It works on clarifying the importance and value of who these women are, what they think, and what they do.[10]

Mujerista theology seeks to provide a platform for Latina grassroots women, taking seriously their religious understandings and practices as a source for theology and challenging theological understandings or church teachings that oppress Latina women.[11] It insists not that liberation is something one person can give another but instead that it is a process by which the oppressed become protagonistas of their own stories, participants in creating a reality different from the oppressive one they are in. Most important, mujerista theology is not a theology exclusively *for* Latinas but a theology *from* Latinas, enabling Latinas to understand the ways they have internalized their own oppression. Practically, mujerista theology is a theology of resistance that aims to help Latinas discover and affirm the presence of God in their communities, as well as the revelation of God in their daily lives.[12]

Although I've resonated with and built many of my ideas from mujerista theology due to its Roman Catholic and Cuban connections, I also understand and want to engage the critiques it has received for the ways it risks a kind of exclusivity or homogeneity that universalizes the Latina/Hispanic experience, often to the advantage of white Latinas. Because of this, I seek to also engage with *feminist intercultural theology* brought forth by María Pilar Aquino, Daisy Machado, Maria José Rosado-Nuñes, and others. For Aquino, feminist intercultural theology adds more nuance to the table. It best names what she calls convivencia (living together) across Latina identities—Catholic, Protestant, Amerindian, African, Latin American, US Latina—as equals in wisdom.[13]

Latina evangélica thought. This framework has helped me see how theology as a whole, including the doctrine of the Trinity and Scripture, intersect with my position as a Latine woman. Latina evangélica thought emphasizes the feminine "Wild Child" of the Trinity, la Espíritu Santa[14] (the Holy Spirit), and the inspiring and inspired word of God in the Bible.[15] The work of Latina evangélicas has reminded me that theology is a communal and collaborative task. Women, particularly women of color, learn from one another's experiences and seek that all, together, are liberated to better serve one another and their neighbors and to live into the freedom promised in la Espíritu Santa.

As I present an abuelita faith (one among many), I am doing so from the shoulders of womanists, mujeristas, intercultural feminists, Latina evangélicas, postcolonial scholars, decolonizing thinkers, and others, continuously gaining insight from their perspectives and theological understandings about God and the world. The work of theology is a work of the people, something we do en conjunto, together. In this way, the image of God is not just individual but collective. We need one another because no one person or one group of people can fully bear all that is God's image. Instead, each culture, people, or group offers a glimpse of a different aspect of the full image of God.

⁓

I "formally" learned about abuelita theology while doing research on César Chávez, the preeminent leader, voice, and public face of the Mexican American civil rights movement of the 1960s.[16] Asian-Latino theologian Robert Chao Romero notes that Chávez's enormous impact on the Mexican community was ultimately started by his grandmother, Mama Tella. In the same way, the role of abuelitas in the lives of many US-based Latines cannot be overstated. Our abuelas are our connection to our culture, our language, and the country that birthed us. They are our wells of wisdom and memories—both traumatic ones and those necessary for survival. For we who are Latines in the US, our abuelitas hold much of our identities, beliefs, traditions, and theologies.

Mama Tella's Catholic faith formed Chávez in the early years of his life.[17] One example was when he received his first Communion. Because the Chávez family lived far outside the city, César was not able to attend regular catechism. Nevertheless, his family took a trip to the city one day to request it from the Anglo priest, who refused, reminding them that they could not take Communion without first receiving "formal" religious training. Chávez's mother, Juana, told the priest to ask César and his sister, Rita, any question from the Catholic catechism to prove they were ready. To the priest's surprise, they answered every question he asked, so he had no choice but to allow them to receive Communion the following day.[18] Chávez, who has been called the Martin Luther King Jr. of the Mexican American community,[19] wouldn't have been who he was without the abuelita theology training he received from Mama Tella.

The story of Mama Tella speaks to the fact that white, Western thought has long monopolized ways of knowing and being, assuming that originating, Indigenous, or immigrant cultures lack aesthetic capacities, intellectual traditions, and/or critical thinking. Dominant culture has historically discredited our communities, labeling them uneducated or, because of other factors like socioeconomic status, assuming they are unable to develop knowledge or articulate their thoughts, particularly in regard to theology.

In his book *After Whiteness*, Black scholar Willie Jennings explains that the image of the educated person in Western culture is that of a white self-sufficient man. His self-sufficiency, Jennings argues, is defined by possession, control, and mastery.[20] Western culture has long made the rules about what is "knowledge" and what is not, positioning themselves as controllers, possessors, masters, and thus as teachers of knowledge. This has resulted not only in homogeneity—"a control that aims for sameness and a sameness that imagines control"[21]—but in the marginalizing or silencing of anyone from outside the white elite academy.

To this end, postcolonial thinker Boaventura de Sousa Santos argues that social justice is not possible without *cognitive justice.* For Santos, cognitive injustice is the failure to recognize the different ways of knowing by which people across the globe live and make meaning of their existence.[22] I echo Santos in urging that we must recover the diversity of ways of being and knowing in the world. While dominant culture says we have nothing to learn from poor or uneducated people, abuelita theology says we have the most to learn from them—from marginalized women like Mama Tella or my own Abuela Evelia.

Not only have the Mama Tellas of the world served as the backbones of our faith, carrying the weight of the César Chávezes of the world, but in doing so, our abuelas have resisted and even shamed the dominant Western notion of "knowledge" that isolates and further marginalizes.

In an interview with Krista Tippett, Robin Wall Kimmerer, a botanist and member of the Citizen Potawatomi Nation, explains that in Indigenous ways of knowing, to know a thing doesn't mean to know something just intellectually, but to know it intuitively. To really know something, you must know it emotionally and spiritually.[23]

"What does it mean to be an educated person?" Kimmerer asks. "It means that you know what your gift is and how to give it on behalf of the land and of the people, just like every single species has its own gift."[24] By this standard, our abuelas are educated beyond measure, offering their gifts to us in ways the academy cannot. The rest of this book will detail some of those ways: how the abuelitas in our midst and in Scripture share their wisdom with us through their hands, their bodies, and their alternative ways of being and knowing.

Abuelita theology is a reality for more than just the Latine community; it has also been expressed by some in the African American community. Hak Joon Lee recounts in *We Will Get to the Promised Land* Martin Luther King Jr.'s intimate relationship with his grandmother, Jennie C. Parks Williams. Lee calls it "the African family characteristic of the abiding presence of maternal bonding."[25] Grandma Jennie played a key role in King's emotional and spiritual formation, instilling in him a strong identity, self-esteem, and mission. King's grandmother "was a strong spiritual force, a bearer of culture, and a pillar of strength in the family."[26] King's bond with his grandmother was so strong that on the two occasions when he thought she had died, he tried to commit suicide. Imagine where our society would be without Grandma Jennie's influence on her grandson's life.

Abuelita theology recognizes and celebrates her life alongside his.

Theologian and civil rights leader Howard Thurman was raised by his grandmother, Nancy Ambrose. He recalls the ways his grandmother served as a rock for their entire community, taking it upon herself to be the one to empower her family—to remind them that despite their circumstances they were God's children. Thurman writes that his grandmother's passion and energy established the ground of personal dignity "so that a profound sense of personal worth could absorb the fear reaction that came with being slaves."[27] His grandmother believed that the Christianity of Jesus appeared as a technique of survival for the oppressed. Through the years, however, it became a religion of the powerful and the dominant, often used as an instrument of oppression. Through his grandmother's influence, Thurman also challenged the notion that oppression was in the mind and life of Jesus.

This, I believe, is what abuelitas possess: a connection to Jesus that empowers, despite the ways dominant culture has attempted to strip them of their dignity, even and especially in the name of Jesus. Thurman's grandmother's teachings about Jesus were instrumental to his ministry and fundamentally shaped his religious sentiments, which eventually birthed *Jesus and the Disinherited*, Thurman's most famous book. It is rumored that King carried a copy of this book in his pocket alongside his Bible.

Many within Native American communities are also intimately acquainted with these experiences—namely, the ways Christianity has been used as an instrument of oppression. Historically, Native peoples have been driven out of their lands, forced to "convert" and be baptized, enslaved, murdered—often in the name of Jesus. Throughout the years of generational trauma and unresolved historical grief, many Native American grandmothers have offered strength to their communities, carrying on cultural knowledge, spiritual awareness, and kinship ties, as community elders and grandparents are often responsible for raising and educating children.[28] Tribal grandmothers often rear grandchildren, and through their age and role as caregivers, older women hold a special status in the community, acting as cultural conservators, exposing their grandchildren to Native American ways of life through ceremonial and informal activities.[29] George Tinker, a theologian and citizen of the Wazhazhe (Osage) Nation, explains that many in his community understand creation as "Grandmother of the Earth": creation is sacred, the earth is a source of life, and creatures are relatives to whom we owe respect and reciprocity.[30] It is this honor that abuelitas are given.

Similarly, Japanese sociologist Yoshinoro Kamo explains that many countries in East Asia, including China, Taiwan, Korea, Japan, and others, have adopted Confucian ethics, which stresses age hierarchy.[31] While most Western nations value individualism and self-reliance, which oftentimes results in ageism, the opposite is true for many Eastern cultures. Not only is a communal mentality upheld, but grandparents, including abuelitas, are among those to be most honored and respected.

Just like the Indigenous communities of North America, my own Indigenous ancestors, the Taínos of the Caribbean, saw women—grandmothers, mothers, sisters, and daughters—as the foundation of society, expressed by the tracing of descent through the female line to a mythical female ancestress. This matrilineal social organization is not uncommon worldwide.[32]

While abuelas serve as the foundation for many US-based Latine peoples, developing a theology of abuelitas isn't unique to the Latine experience.

<hr/>

Abuelita theology stems from the reality that in Latine religious culture, matriarchal figures such as abuelitas preserve and pass along religious traditions, beliefs, practices, and spirituality. They function as "live-in ministers," particularly because the privilege to receive "formal" religious instruction is often unavailable. Thus, abuelitas are the functional priestesses and theologians in our familias. The theologies we have inherited from these overlooked women have given us a firm foundation to live out our faith and demonstrate love in the world. "These wise women taught us about the power of prophetic words and the responsibility we have to seek and hear them," writes Loida I. Martell-Otero. "They did not simply pass on *el evangelio* (the gospel) as a set of accepted dogmatic statements. They nurtured us with a keen sense of the Spirit's ability to create anew."[33]

The teachings of our abuelitas were our starting points, but we continue on in an ongoing and communal effort to critically discern aspects of our inherited traditions that have been colonized.[34] I offer this book in the hope that together not only will we embody a community eager to recognize overlooked and unnamed abuelita theologians in our midst, but we will seek to live out abuelita faith in our everyday lives.

Abuelita faith isn't just a cultural reality but a biblical one as well. Scripture testifies to the power and influence of grandmothers among the people of God. For years I overlooked this detail because I hadn't been trained to recognize the importance or value of women in the Bible. For example, I wasn't taught to let my gaze linger on the women included in most of Paul's letter introductions—or to ask what it meant that they were there in the first place. Similarly, many people in church weren't taught to understand the way this letter writing process worked in the first century—the weight of someone sponsoring, delivering, and reading (which at that time would have been akin to preaching) a letter once it was delivered to a house church (as with Phoebe, the deacon whom Paul commends at the end of his extended treatise in Romans).

In the same way, I overlooked the introduction to Paul's second letter to Timothy until one day it caught my attention, affirming my curiosity and conviction of the importance of both abuelitas and the faith of my ancestors. In this short passage, Paul says: "I'm grateful to God, whom I serve with a good conscience *as my ancestors did*. I constantly remember you in my prayers day and night. When I remember your tears, I long to see you so that I can be filled with happiness. I'm reminded of your authentic faith, *which first lived in your grandmother Lois and your mother Eunice*. I'm sure that this faith is also inside you" (2 Tim. 1:3–5, emphasis mine).

Here Paul names the power and importance of abuelita theology.

By acknowledging Timothy's faith (a faith birthed from his abuelita and his mamá), Paul honors the two women, puts their names in ink so that they are forever remembered—canonized, if you will. He acknowledges that their faith is a communal faith that takes seriously the impact of not just the people who came before him but the *women* who formed and shaped him. This powerful affirmation changed the course of my life, reminding me that abuelita theology has been around for centuries. It also led me to retrain and recenter my thinking, allowing me to see new characters and new insights calling to me from the pages of this sacred book.

I often wonder what Abuela Lois and Mama Eunice's faith looked like. How did they live it out? Were they dedicated to serving the community like Tabitha? Were they leading house churches like Lydia did or instructing leaders like Priscilla did? Did they speak truth to power like Nancy Ambrose or Grandma Jennie?

I stand on the shoulders of my abuela's popular Catholicism. For the majority of my childhood I attended mass, catechism classes, and confession, and I received my first Communion and confirmation into the Catholic Church. After I made my transition to Protestantism in my early twenties, however, I began to believe some of the evangelical tropes about Abuela's faith: particularly, that it is "works based" because it engages practices like upholding the sacraments and attending confession. I began to believe that engaging with symbols like those of the saints was "idol worship." Those first few years as a new evangelical, I cried so many tears of despair for Abuela's salvation, because I was told to believe her faith wasn't authentic, that she needed to be saved, converted.

I internalized the hyperindividualistic view of faith and salvation, believing the notion that following Jesus is simply a personal decision that I make "in my heart." I bought into the idea that my spirituality is private, that my spiritual growth has absolutely nothing to do with my community, my ancestors—the cloud of witnesses, those I knew directly and indirectly—as well as the countless number of people who have influenced me or even those I myself have influenced. To this end Palestinian scholar Jean Zaru says, "Many argue that one's faith, or one's spirituality, is one's own private affair. I disagree, for spirituality includes all the dimensions of human, personal, and societal living that combine to make human life human—the measure of the fullness of God's gift."[35]

I often wonder, In the demonizing or disregarding of other expressions of Christian faith, have evangelicals forgotten that the church, rightly understood, is a communion of saints—not just here on earth but also in heaven? The saints are like "open treasure-houses accessible to all, like flowing fountains at which everyone can drink. Nothing in the Communion of Saints is private, although everything is personal."[36] The communion of saints has enriched my theological imagination, particularly when it comes to my ancestors and las madres of the faith, the women throughout history who have gone before us paving the way, building their own tables, and offering a perspective of the divine, without which our faith would be lacking.

Las madres and madrinas of the faith are the often-ignored women who make up the cloud of witnesses alluded to in the book of Hebrews. They have empowered us—from women like Deborah, the prophet and judge who helped lead Israel to victory alongside Jael, to women like Junia, a notable apostle in the New Testament church. There are also women whose work has proved invaluable, like Paula of Rome, who established monasteries and churches and translated the Bible from Hebrew to Greek alongside the famous Latin scholar Jerome.

There are still others, like Teresa Urrea, who played an important role in Mexico as a saint and a curandera (healer) and who also fought for justice for Indigenous peoples. Or María Elena Moyano, an Afro-Peruvian community organizer who was assassinated in the early 1990s for her activism. Or Josefa Llanes Escoda, a Filipina advocate of women's suffrage who fought for peace during the Japanese occupation of the Philippines. The list is endless.

My antepasadas illuminated my faith only after I invited my culture, my upbringing, and my identity as a Latina into dialogue with who I am as a person of faith. Like Timothy's, my faith was handed down to me from my abuelita, complete with the memories of St. Dominic Catholic Church in Miami, where I was first baptized, where I first received the Eucharist, and where I watched Abuela sing in the choir every Sunday. Instead of disconnecting me from these important parts of my spirituality, the divine has allowed them to give me a more robust and integrated understanding of my faith and myself.

My efforts in presenting this theology are to go back to the basics, to envision a grassroots movement in which abuelitas are at the center of the narrative. My hope is that those without power or privilege in society, many of whom hold our families together, would be highly honored by all. In digging deep into their stories, I hope that alternate forms of knowledge, embodied knowledge passed on from our ancestors, would be highlighted as gifts endowed by God. Lastly, my desire is that the stories of these women in Scripture and beyond illuminate something new in us so that when we see those on the margins living life en la lucha, in the struggle, we would be drawn to their experiences and drink from their wells overflowing with sabiduría, wisdom, about the divine.

3

A Sabiduría That Heals

If you're familiar with any aspect of the Latine community, chances are you've heard one of our abuelitas' common refranos ("refrains," or more accurately translated, "proverbs" or "sayings"). While each Latine culture is unique, there's still a certain thread that binds us together: our abuelitas carry a wisdom that knows no bounds. We don't always know where the refranos of our abuelitas come from, but they've shaped us and our collective wisdom. Oftentimes, they're learned through lived experiences. And lived experience is key; as I learned growing up, "El diablo sabe más por viejo que por diablo." (The devil is wise more because he's old than because he's the devil.)

Refranos have gotten us through life. Perhaps they've helped us learn how to navigate friendships in middle school: "Dime con quien andas, y te diré quien eres." (Tell me who you spend time with, and I'll tell you who you are.) Or "Mejor sola que mal acompañada." (Better alone than with bad company.) Perhaps they've even helped us evaluate people: "Perro que ladra no muerde." (Barking dogs don't bite—in other words, people talk more than they act.) Our abuelas ooze wisdom that is both learned and embodied, knowledge gained from oral traditions and intuitions that take shape in lo cotidiano. I still live by "A quien madruga, Dios lo ayuda." (God helps those who get up early—a proverb similar to "The early bird gets the worm.") Abuela's hard-work ethic condensed into a memorable life lesson has formed me.

The wisdom of our abuelas heals us, whether it's the reminder that "sana sana colita de rana, si no sanas hoy sanarás mañana" (heal, heal, little frog's tail, if you don't heal today, you'll heal tomorrow), which means that healing takes time, or the reminder that "el que no llora no mama" (the one who doesn't cry, doesn't drink milk), which means that if we want something, we must ask for it. Most of their refranos live in our bodies and engage our senses. To this day, even with Abuela's old age and dementia, she utters a few of her sayings when I visit. Her favorite is "Manos frías, amor para un día. Manos calientes, amor para siempre." She'll say this as she grasps my often cold hands, laying a soft kiss on the top of them, reminding me that cold hands mean love for a day, but warm hands mean love forever. And she's right—my hands in hers are instantly warm, the sign of a forever love.

Through their refranos, among other things, our abuelitas have offered a path of spiritual wisdom, of conocimiento. The ways they engage the world provide us a spiritual inquiry that is formed by the way they engage their faith in their day-to-day lives, including their art making, their healing, their dance, and their "inclusionary politics."[1]

Our abuelas also gain wisdom to pass along, in part through how they pray and read and apply Scripture. I often hear story after story of abuelas committing hours to reading the Bible and praying. Most engage without commentaries and without seminary education. In many ways, their lived experiences and the ways they have ensured everyday survival inform their spiritual practices.

When many of us with varying levels of privilege interact with the Bible's stories, particularly those of Jesus engaging with marginalized women, we often have to force ourselves into the narrative. I wonder if much of our abuelitas' theological insight comes from the fact that they can see themselves clearly in the story. They don't need to stretch to imagine what it would be like to be the Samaritan woman or the persistent widow. Many of our abuelas know those stories intimately not only because they've committed to studying them and their lessons but because oftentimes those stories are about them. What they pass on to us is a knowledge about God that many of us spend our lives trying to obtain from books and conferences. Our abuelitas may be "uneducated" by the dominant culture's standards, but they possess PhDs in prayer and Bible interpretation. They may not be ordained as official priests or pastors, but they've been playing those roles behind the scenes forever, noticed and called by God.

―――――――

The journey of spiritual conocimiento, of inner and divine exploration, that many of us find ourselves on is a task of going backward, of reaching into the past to reclaim the wisdom of our abuelas and our ancestors. I believe part of this wisdom includes their understanding of the interconnectedness of all people, nature, and God.

When I think about the work of conocimiento and the process of reaching back to Abuela's embodied wisdom, I remember how she saw all things as intertwined. I think of her mango trees that provided nourishment for our familia as well as shelter for the animals that came to lie underneath them. I think of the pregnant stray cats that would break through the screen of our small duplex, clawing through the open windows in order to find a safe space inside of our home to give birth. We always had newly birthed kittens en la casita, in the shed, behind our house. After the cats gave birth, Abuela would clean them and detach their umbilical cords, and the mami cat would let her, exposing her belly in trust. Abuela would tell me that she learned how to do that en el campo, in the countryside. She'd find lizard eggs en la casita and call me to come see: "¡Katy! ¡Katy! ¡Mira!" (Katy! Katy! Look!) And we'd take care of them until they hatched, protecting them against predators. I've learned that lizards are sacred to the Taíno people and play an important role in their story of origin. I think Abuela carried that knowledge within her body; perhaps she knew the sacred sabiduría of our ancestors intimately.

If we are to regain this sabiduría, wisdom, we must reclaim and reconstruct our spirituality, built on the backs of those who came before us, especially those who were overlooked or silenced. This work becomes poignant when we remember the silencing of women's voices, especially within an imperial Christianity. An early example dates all the way back to the fourth century, when the Roman emperor Constantine received in a dream the instruction to "conquer" by the sign of the cross of Jesus. As a result, his armies "smashed through to victory," replacing all "pagan standards" with images of a cross and the first two letters of Christ's name, thus wielding the cross and sword together and fusing church and state.[2]

Shortly after Constantine issued an edict of toleration legalizing Christianity throughout the empire, the first wars of an imperial church against so-called pagans and their practices were instigated. Throughout the following century, edicts ordered the persecution, destruction, and defacement of all that was not "Christian" in the institutional and imperial sense of the word. This included not only traditions and practices but libraries and healing centers.[3] One city that was targeted in this ancient purge was Alexandria, Egypt. Alexandria was a hub of ancient knowledge from places like Mesopotamia, Babylon, Syria, Persia, India, and Greece, and from the Egyptian culture that had flourished along the Nile. Alexandria contained sacred materials, libraries, and centers of learning by which the population flourished.

In 392 CE, a riot by Christian mobs destroyed Alexandria's most important center of scholarship, which held the city's sacred library. After the destruction of this learning center came the violent murder of Alexandria's most learned woman, a philosopher, mathematician, and prominent thinker and teacher by the name of Hypatia. In 415 CE, a Christian mob accused her of being a witch, tore out her eyes, dragged her corpse through the streets of the city, and burned her remains.[4] Her body and the wisdom that she carried within her were ripped to shreds. Her death at the hands of zealous Christians symbolizes the murder of our Native abuelas and the squelching of their wisdom.

Violence ensued across the centuries as the cross and the sword became one. What had begun as a small group of Jesus followers selling their possessions, sharing what they had in common, and living a life of harmony, humility, and self-sacrifice had turned into a movement of power—Jesus's cross symbolizing greed and destruction.

After Columbus's arrival to the Americas, advanced mathematics, astronomical observations, herbal medicine, and other genius practices of Indigenous civilizations were marked as evil and set for destruction. And yet many popular beliefs and practices within modern-day Christianity were born from these Indigenous and so-called pagan practices.

For example, my social media feed is chock-full of posts from Christian women posing alongside essential oil starter kits that promise to uplift moods, relieve stress, help with sleep, and provide physical and mental healing through the dabbing of concoctions that contain healing properties found in eucalyptus, lavender, and other all-natural herbs. These "potions" that serve as modern-day, natural healing agents date back five thousand years, originating in ancient Egypt (where Hypatia was deemed a witch and murdered by Christians). Healing remedies through herbal medicine were part of spiritual practices in the ancient world and were foundational to popular spirituality.[5] Herbal medicine included things like rubbing, dabbing, and even inhaling herbs for calming and healing effects, not too different from current practices.[6]

During the colonial period, these forms of African spiritual practices spread to the Americas through the millions of African people who were captured and brought by Spain as slaves in accordance with the Spanish church. Part of European colonization involved the attempt to tame and even exterminate these forms of spirituality and replace them with a more "civilized," Western one—namely, Christianity. It's no surprise that the history of the church since then, and particularly modern Western evangelicalism, has not only rejected popular forms of African and Indigenous spirituality but has also regarded them as demonic. But what can be said about Western Christianity when it adapts a key part of Indigenous and African spiritual tradition while simultaneously demonizing the very culture, people, and expressions of faith it comes from?

These healing potions turned "essential oils" stem from the embodied knowledge of our ancestors, centuries-old abuelitas whose relationships with the land and the divine within it have proved invaluable.[7] As Tejana poet Carolina Hinojosa-Cisneros once wrote on a Facebook post, "Ancestral wealth is deeper than imaginary borders and complicated histories."[8] The more I seek to decolonize, even my readings of Scripture, the more in love I fall with the mysterious grand Creator who imbued our ancestors with embodied knowledge. A God of healing, of curanderismo.

The Bible has a lot to say about sabiduría (wisdom), *khokmah* in Hebrew and *sophia* in Greek. In Hebrew, the word *khokmah* implies not an intellectual wisdom but skill or applied knowledge—the kind of wisdom a skilled artisan who excels at their craft possesses, an embodied wisdom that creates and sustains.

The first full biblical personification of wisdom appears in the book of Proverbs.[9] Proverbs encourages God's people: "Get wisdom; get understanding. . . . Don't abandon her, and she will guard you. Love her, and she will protect you" (4:5–6). In Christian tradition we believe this wisdom comes from la Espíritu Santa, the Holy Spirit.

The Hebrew Scriptures use the word *spirit* to refer to the Holy Spirit eighty-four times. Of those eighty-four occurrences, seventy-five of them refer to the Holy Spirit in feminine terms. For example, in Genesis 1:2, where the term *Spirit of God* first appears, it is in feminine form. In Judges, the spirit is always feminine. And in Proverbs, the Wisdom of God, which much of Christian tradition understands to be the Holy Spirit, is personified as a woman. In fact, this is one of the greatest ways that God is referred to in feminine terms. Throughout Scripture, Wisdom (God) is a she.

Puerto Rican theologian Mayra Rivera points to the fact that wisdom, or Sophia, as she names her, stands out as a rarity in the Bible because of her gender. "In a community in which identity is defined in reference to its male members, doesn't the fact that Sophia is a female make her an odd image of authority?"[10] asks Rivera. In Proverbs, Sophia stands out in the street, in the public square, at the entrance of the city gates, crying out to those who will listen (1:20–21). This is a striking contrast with the "competent wife" of Proverbs 31 whose husband is the one who is known in the city gates (vv. 10, 23). Instead of her husband, Sophia stands there herself, putting her at the crossroads of "proper" gender roles.[11] Lady Wisdom is atrevida, daring. She is a woman who crosses borders, imaginary and fixed, like la Espíritu Santa.

I wonder if the evangelicalism of dominant culture often represses the Holy Spirit not only because of the ways she is characterized as a she but also because she cannot be tamed.

Zaida Maldonado Pérez calls the Holy Spirit the Wild Child of the Trinity—untamable, full of possibilities and creative potential, wonderfully elusive yet always fully present. She is the *ruakh*, the breath, of God who is always "going native."[12] When the day of Pentecost arrived and all who were present encountered the Holy Spirit, they each spoke and heard the gospel in their "native language" (Acts 2:8). Who can say this "native" wisdom born from the beginning of time and introduced in Genesis 1 as hovering over the earth, isn't the same wisdom that guided our ancestors in their knowledge, their ways of being and knowing—from astronomical cycles that directed their crop production to the herbal potions that engaged their healing. Or is the Eurocentric "wisdom," which murdered, enslaved, and destroyed, the only *sophia* that remains?

There are many unnamed women who possess wisdom in Scripture, but two overlooked "wise women," mujeres sabias, in particular stick out to me. If we would learn to look around our world in spaces least expected, in between and within the stories of Abraham, Moses, and the other patriarchs, we would stumble upon more wise women.

They've always been there. They're still here.

The first of these wise women is found in 2 Samuel 14. Her name is lost within the details of David's story. In the narrative, David's general Joab sends for a wise woman, a mujer sabia, in Tekoa to come to Jerusalem to speak to David about his son Absalom, who killed his brother Amnon in order to avenge the rape of their sister Tamar. Absalom has been in exile for three years, and Joab feels it is time that David reconcile with his son because he "could see that the king's mind was on Absalom"

(v. 1). So Joab has the wise woman put on mourning garments and act as someone grieving for the dead. Joab then tells her to tell King David a fabricated story about her being a widow with two sons, one of whom killed the other and is now in danger of being murdered by the rest of the clan, mirroring the story of David's sons Absalom and Amnon. After David gives orders to protect her son, the wise woman turns and accuses him of having incriminated himself. After further conversation, David heeds her words and allows Absalom to return to Jerusalem.

I wonder, Who is this mujer sabia? What's her story? The fact that Joab sent for this woman, bringing her from another city to perform this specific task, proves that the wise woman of Tekoa is not just anybody. Perhaps her vocational role as a wise woman is one that was sought after. We can assume her wisdom was known throughout the region. What made her wise? I wonder if she got her wisdom from her abuela, or if her lived experience gained her the title "wise woman." How did Joab know she was in Tekoa anyway? Tekoa was known for its olives and its peculiar fruit called "sycamore fruit," a valuable plant for bees. Thus, ancient tradition makes this place proverbial for both oil (derived from olives) and honey[13]—a sacred element that God gifts to God's people throughout the Scriptures. Perhaps this mujer sabia's wisdom came from the land; her knowledge had roots in the dirt.

I'm curious about the authority this mujer possessed, considering the fact that King David not only listened to her but heeded her advice and her rebuke.[14] As I mentioned, the wise woman is responding to the story of Tamar. After Amnon rapes Tamar, the text says that David "got very angry, but he refused to punish his son Amnon" (2 Sam. 13:21). Perhaps David's disregard of sexual assault is part of what led to his son's death. Thus, some have wondered if the editor of 2 Samuel is trying to mirror the interaction between David and the wise woman after that of David and the prophet Nathan, who indicts David for his assault on Bathsheba two chapters earlier. This is due to the fact that the exchange and circumstances are similar. If so, why is Nathan often talked about but never la mujer sabia, whose words lead David to action by indirect means?

Her shrewd speech is unlike any other. She juxtaposes hints of guilt with declarations of elaborate praise, putting the king in an awkward position, keeping herself safe while coercing him. Some argue this is an impressive feat, considering the mortality rate of those around the king during this time.[15] Perhaps this mujer sabia also had her own refranos—her own ways of seeing and understanding the world. Many believe that the prophets Jeremiah and Amos lived in Tekoa and that Amos was even born there. Perhaps they received their wisdom from this abuelita, this ancestor who led them to say, "Let justice roll down like waters" (Amos 5:24) and "Do what is just and right; rescue the oppressed from the power of the oppressor. Don't exploit or mistreat the refugee, the orphan, and the widow" (Jer. 22:3).

A few chapters later we meet another mujer sabia. In the narrative of 2 Samuel 20, tensions are high between the southern tribe of Judah and the ten northern tribes of Israel after David has suppressed Absalom's revolt. Sheba, a Benjaminite from the north, calls for the northerners to rebel or secede. He then flees to the north to take refuge in Abel, where Joab chases him down. As Joab's men attack the wall at Abel in an attempt to get into the city, a "wise woman" calls out for negotiations to save her city. As with the woman at Tekoa, Joab responds to her in a way that honors her position and authority.

In her speech, she accuses Joab of seeking to kill "a city that is one of Israel's mothers." "People used to say long ago: 'Ask your question at Abel,' and that settled the matter," she says (2 Sam. 20:18–19). Some argue that the rhetoric this mujer sabia uses in her speech is "a masterpiece of manipulation."[16] She links her city's reputation for being one of wise counsel with her own claim of being one of the "peaceful and faithful in Israel." "Why would you annihilate the LORD's inheritance?" she asks (20:19). Her question makes Joab defensive, and he answers that he would never annihilate or destroy such a thing. He asks only then for Sheba's head. This request ends up sparing the entire city, thanks to la mujer sabia's intercession.

Now, a decolonized lens would question the beheading of *any* person, but as we will see in later chapters, women must often acquiesce to questionable actions in order to survive. Given the context, this unnamed woman ensures the safety not only of her family but of her entire city by the shrewdness of her speech. Like the story of her counterpart in Tekoa, this story of a wise woman attests to what must have been a regularized public role for women, at least through the early period of the Israelite monarchy.[17]

In other words, during this time, ancient Israel had "official" abuelita theologians.

An often overlooked antepasada in Mexican tradition is Sor Juana Inés de la Cruz, who used her wisdom to challenge the church's colonialist and patriarchal ideology in the seventeenth century. She did so through her theological writings, poems, and plays, and even her villancicos (worship hymns), which she used to sing social justice–themed songs.[18] Juana's commitment to learning was such that as a young girl she tried to convince her mom to dress her up in boys' clothes in an effort to attain higher learning. When this didn't work, she resolved to teach herself, even disciplining herself by cutting off chunks of her own hair when she was slacking.[19]

After being invited to join the viceregal court to become a lady-in-waiting, Juana used her position to write poetry and plays that defended women's rights to education. When given the chance to marry, Juana chose to become a nun instead, as doing so would secure her decision to devote her life to study. As a nun, Juana continued to write plays, poetry, and theological essays that drew much criticism by male religious authorities.[20]

After challenging the Christology of a renowned Portuguese Jesuit theologian, Antonio de Viera, Juana was publicly chastised by the bishop of Puebla, and male authorities requested her study be forbidden. This led her to write a series of essays defending her right as a woman to study Scripture, claiming her love of learning came from God. This was monumental for her time. Robert Chao Romero explains that "in a day and age when the Catholic Church ruled with an iron male hand and all the authority and tools of the Spanish Inquisition, Sor Juana fought mightily with her pen, with little to no political or spiritual support."[21]

The wisdom that Juana possessed was too intimidating, too suspect for the religious patriarchy. Under the pressure of the bishop of Puebla, Juana was forced to sell her library, which contained her intellectual knowledge bound in books. The weight of persecution became too much for her to bear, as she also signed a public statement of repentance. Her last year was lived in penance and quiet reflection. Juana symbolizes the embodied wisdom that our abuelitas possess. She fought a lifelong battle for the liberation of the mujeres who would come after her, and like Hypatia and so many others, her wisdom was silenced.

Similarly, Afro-Brazilian author and abolitionist Maria Firmina dos Reis was an ancestral madre who used her words to speak of the evil of slavery. Reis was born on the São Luís island in Maranhão in 1825, three years after Brazil declared independence from Portugal. Not only did Reis found Brazil's first free and mixed school, but her novel *Úrsula* is known as the work that truly initiated Afro-Brazilian literature. In her writings, Reis addresses Black identity in a way that was unique for her time and made her Afro-Brazilian characters the subjects of their own discourse, retelling history from their own viewpoint and embodying values like their beliefs in God and their experiences.[22]

Reis's story is both inspiring and heartbreaking. Although she was such an influential figure in her time, her story is often overlooked and ignored. She was a monumental writer, educator, and composer—a woman who dared to call out the evils of the dominating culture. What I find so special about Reis is that her wisdom was born from her mother's and grandmother's influence, as she never received formal education but obtained most of her knowledge at home.

There have always been wise women, and even though many of them go unnamed in Scripture, my hope is that they would not go unnoticed any longer, that their wisdom would be celebrated. Whether our abuelitas have official roles like in the ancient world (which men of power like King David and his general Joab submitted to) or unofficial roles (like the wise women in our familias who pass on their words of wisdom gained through their lived experiences and their resolute commitment to their faith), we must return to seeing and honoring our abuelitas. Perhaps these "wise women" possessed a sabiduría that came from la Espíritu Santa, the spirit "gone native" that is intimately connected to the divine, the land, and its living things. Like Sor Juana, Maria Firmina dos Reis, and the wise women of 2 Samuel, who sought justice for an entire people, so our abuelas often live lives in which the well-being of those around them is of utmost importance to them.

The wisdom of our abuelas comes from our ancestors, perhaps even the unnamed from Tekoa and Abel, and that wisdom is passed on to us—a sabiduría that heals.

4

Mujeres of Exodus

The night of Papi's exodus from Cuba, he boarded a lancha (a small raft) with a few other people to head to the States. He never imagined it would be the last time his feet would stand on the soil of his island. I envision him with his heart pounding in his chest and sweat dripping from his pitch-black hair over his caramel skin as he takes one last look at Abuela before pushing off the wet sand, resting his gaze on the shore as it disappears into the dark night. I try to imagine Papi all the time. Although he was my grandfather, I never had the chance to meet him, to call him Abuelo, so I call him Papi instead, according to his memory, like the rest of the familia.

Most who left la isla after the revolution were certain they would return, positive they would get another chance to dig their toes in the white sand, to walk through the streets of Havana, or to sit around la mesa en el campo (the table in the country) with friends, the salty breeze offering a cool respite from the warm tropical climate. They thought political unrest would subside after a few months and they'd get to return home. But for Papi—and most others—that moment never came.

That journey in the pitch-black ocean without knowledge of what lurked underneath or what was to come, or when he'd see our familia again, was enough to kill Papi years later. Some family members say his health problems began with his kidneys after he developed an infection from holding his bladder the entire trip to Florida. Rumor has it he refused to relieve himself in front of the only woman traveling in the lancha with them. Others say the stress and the trauma of the entire situation—the revolution, a midnight escape, the exile—is what killed him.

Perhaps the ocean knows—those stories may be wading in the Florida Straits. All we know is that his heart gave out a couple years after he arrived.

Papi's first year here, he worked at a grocery store as a carnicero (a butcher) in an effort to save up enough money to fly the rest of my family from Cuba: Abuela, Mom, and my aunt and uncle, Mama and Kiko. While life shifted in the States, Abuela and her children waited under the weight of uncertainty. Finally, a year later, they were able to make their exodus. They packed their bags with only essential belongings and crossed the ocean for the last time.

The ocean that separates me from my ancestors holds painful memories and sacred stories. Often called the Corridor of Death, those ninety miles of water between Cuba and Florida have swallowed up refugee bodies by the thousands. Still others have had their lives transformed by those very same waters.

Potawatomi author Kaitlin Curtice writes, "Water can be a dangerous thing, but water is also the lifeblood of us all. It is why flood stories are so powerful and so sacred; the earth gets destroyed by water, and it gets rebuilt by that same water as it gives life to everything again."[1]

Growing up I held a deep respect for the water, and I sought her nourishment regularly. When visiting the edge of the Atlantic,

I remained close to her shore, never wading too far out lest she carry me away with her power and strength—too much for my body to fight against.

My city's tropical climate meant that I was regularly met with the water that was born in the clouds—dripping its healing powers onto the soil, creating new life, making our gardens lush and green. The hurricanes that form over water also paid us regular visits, often flooding our homes and destroying all our belongings.

Water is a powerful force. It heals and nourishes; it devastates and destroys. It also tells stories of exodus.

Many marginalized peoples have often found both themselves and God within the exodus story in the Bible. One of the leading voices of liberation theology, Archbishop Óscar Romero, used the Israelite exodus to speak life to the poor in El Salvador, reminding his people that the people of God suffered hunger, mistreatment, and oppression until one day they were liberated. Martin Luther King Jr. spoke of God's heart to free God's people from slavery in his mobilizing efforts during the civil rights movement. Through the story of the Israelites enslaved in Egypt, we learn about a God who chooses to engage humanity in a journey from subjugation and bondage to political and social liberation.

While the exodus narrative is important in considering a theology of liberation, I want to be sensitive to the ways it has been critiqued by decolonizing thinkers who ask nuanced questions about notions of conquest in Scripture. For example, in his essay "Canaanites, Cowboys, and Indians," Native American theologian Robert Warrior argues that the exodus promotes a conquering narrative ultimately premised on the genocide of the Indigenous people of the promised land: the Canaanites, the Hittites, and others (Exod. 3:8).[2] Similarly, Palestinian

Christian Jean Zaru asks, "How, one wonders, could a God of justice and compassion command the slaughter of one people to accomplish the liberation of another?" She argues that the life of Jesus is proof that God would not command such a thing, leading her to propose that perhaps "the God of that portion of the biblical account is the God of people's consciousness and perception rather than the God who really is." This is due, according to Zaru, to the Israelites' concept of being the "chosen people."[3]

As I seek to be a responsible and holistic interpreter and reader of the biblical text, I remain sensitive to these critiques and suggestions, aware of how a biblical story might play both a liberating and a triggering role for different communities devastated by imperialism. As Warrior urges, we need to be more aware of the way ideas such as those in conquest narratives have made their way into the consciousness and ideology of US Americans.[4] Decolonized thinking seeks to read the exodus story through Canaanite eyes alongside Israelite eyes—to be honest, to name the tension. It doesn't mean we will have all of the answers to the complicated questions that might arise; it just means we must be willing to wrestle with the text and the ways the text has been used both for good and for evil.

To this end, I echo the words of womanist biblical scholar Wilda Gafney: "I don't run from a fight or a hard text or a fight with a hard text. I believe in wrestling the bruising words until I squeeze a blessing out of them, no matter how down and dirty it gets or how out of joint I get."[5] This brings to mind Genesis 32, when Jacob wrestles with "the angel," who many believe to be God Godself. While wrestling, the unknown "man" disjoints Jacob's hip and then tells him to let him go. "I won't let you go until you bless me," Jacob responds (v. 26). The man then asks Jacob for his name, and when he tells him, the man replies, "Your name won't be Jacob any longer, but Israel, because you struggled with God and with men and won" (v. 27). Like Gafney (and Jacob), I, too, seek to wrestle with the sacred until I squeeze a blessing out of it, despite how disjointed I might get.

For many marginalized communities who identify with Israel, the thought of leaving Egypt is coupled with a narrative of hope: arriving at the promised land, or the mountaintop, as King referred to it. Liberation theologian Gustavo Gutiérrez says concerning this, "The promised land is not simply a new country; it is also the gift of a radically new situation."[6] Ordinary people are forced to make extraordinary decisions to leave the oppressive contexts they find themselves in, in search of something better, a new reality. This has been true for people throughout history and was true for the Israelites in Egypt.

The first person we typically associate the exodus narrative with is Moses, and with good reason. Moses holds multiple identities within himself: an adoptive son and a privileged Hebrew living in the Egyptian courts. In the first part of his story, he stands up for the cause of his people (perhaps too little, too late) and is misunderstood, forcing him into his own exile before the Exile. He flees out of fear for his life, lives with a speech impediment, and is sent back by God to the people who rejected him to liberate them from the powers of empire.

Moses is a relatable character. He trusts God but also deals with insecurity, fear, and impostor syndrome. But the story of the liberation of the Israelites doesn't begin with him. Like all movements, it begins with a faithful few, and like many movements within modern history, it begins with mujeres.

Within Cuban history, women played an important behind-the-scenes role in opposition movements against Fulgencio Batista, the right-wing military dictator who was backed by the US government for his anti-Communist and probusiness views. His corruption set the scene for the Cuban Revolution led by Fidel Castro in 1959. Batista's regime was so oppressive that many

Cubans initially supported Castro and his left-wing policies, looking to him to overturn corruption on the island. The early days of the revolution set the stage for what was to come.

While men were considered the leaders of this period because of their role in the public domain, women proved to be essential, participating in many influential movements that included protestor phone chains, rumor campaigns, "flash" protests, patriotic street theaters, boycotts, and more.[7] "Housewives" played an active role in the urban underground as messengers and spies, using their homes as a cover for their actions of dissent and resistance. These women used their bedrooms for creating, storing, and distributing things like protest letters and opposition news. Phone chains and rumor campaigns became such powerful tools that government officials passed an emergency decree specifying severe punishment for people who engaged in spreading them.[8] As violence grew, homes doubled as shelters for movement militants identified by the police, with the most famous safe houses often run by women. Churches also became popular political sites during the resistance because Cuban church attendance was predominantly female.

Although these forms of protest were nonconfrontational, they encompassed a deep sense of civic activism in a domain that women could fully engage. This became known as passive resistance and could have culminated in the shutting down of the entire city—"ciudad muerta" (dead city), they called it. Women dominated in these forms of collaboration and strategizing, with urban movements pioneering creative tactics of gender-inclusive protest and consciousness raising that helped discredit the dictatorship. Women in all spheres of life—but especially those in the home—proved to be important actors as the insurrection grew.[9]

Around the same time in history, across the Florida Straits, Black women were acting as the backbone of the civil rights movement and the event that ignited it—namely, the Montgomery Bus Boycott. Ultimately, the boycott was successful because of behind-the-scenes organizing by the Women's Political Council (WPC) led by Jo Ann Robinson. As WPC president, Robinson made bus desegregation one of the organization's top priorities after she was verbally attacked by a bus driver for sitting five rows from the front of a nearly empty bus.[10] Following Rosa Parks's arrest, Robinson led the WPC in planning a bus boycott by copying tens of thousands of leaflets and distributing them across the city. This led to what we know as the key event, the boycott, that began on December 5, 1955, when fifty thousand people walked off city buses in defiance of existing conditions, which were demeaning, humiliating, and intolerable. For thirteen months they refused to ride buses unless conditions were changed to meet their approval. Finally, in December 1956, thirteen long months after the boycott began, the federal courts ordered the buses integrated.[11] This extraordinary success was accomplished by the struggle, support, and commitment of a group of Black women.

The details of these histories are often sidelined as "women's history" the same way theology done by Black, Brown, and Asian thinkers is deemed "contextual" and often condensed into a single lecture in a theology course or a paragraph in a history book. But the more we study the underside of history, the more we cannot deny the power of women on the margins. It's no wonder the dominating culture can be so quick to silence and dismiss us.

The story of Israel's exodus from Egypt begins with a desperate mother and includes a group of women whose resistance efforts served as the backbone for liberation. While Moses takes center stage in the first chapter of Exodus as the child who escaped Pharaoh's order to kill Hebrew sons, one particular mujer—whose name is often unrecognized—plays a pivotal role: his mamá, Jochebed. Jochebed made the bold decision to send her son off on an unaccompanied journey in the hope that it would secure his future.

But before learning of Jochebed in Exodus, we meet two other women: Shiphrah and Puah, the midwives who also made brave, dangerous decisions that set the scene for liberation.

The first chapter of Exodus is situated between Joseph's death in Egypt (Gen. 50) and the birth of Moses (Exod. 2). Looking back to the patriarchal narratives of Genesis 12–50, we see that they conclude with the descendants of Israel living comfortably in Egypt as a large family group. Israel's political and economic fortunes were secure until the death of Joseph, who had been appointed by Pharaoh as governor. But because of Joseph's death, the fate of the descendants of Israel hung in the balance.

By the time the story begins, many years have passed and the family has grown to become a large nation whose people are now held as slaves in Egypt, the ruling empire of the Levant. The area that the Israelites were settled in was the well-watered eastern section of the Nile Delta, called Goshen. Because of its proximity to Asia and because two major routes between Egypt and Syria-Palestine passed through it, Goshen served as a haven for Asiatic immigrants and a gateway through which travelers, traders, and invaders passed on their way to Egypt.[12] This made the area strategically important for the security of Egypt and prompted Pharaoh to put pressure on the Israelites living there.

The Israelites remained in Goshen long after the famine that had driven them out of Canaan was over. Perhaps they remained there out of comfort, giving themselves an opportunity to prosper, multiply, and form a coherent society, preserving their identity through the memory of their antepasados, the patriarchs and matriarchs, and their covenant relationship with God.[13]

Concerned by Israel's growth, Pharaoh put a decree in place to curb Israelite reproduction, first by forced labor. However, the text says that "the more they were oppressed, the more they grew and spread, so much so that the Egyptians started to look at the Israelites with disgust and dread" (Exod. 1:12).

What's interesting is that up until this point, only the men are mentioned in the story, but as we all know, the actual duty of producing healthy children (who Pharaoh worried would take over) falls to women. Women are the ones who carry children to term, deliver them, and raise them to adulthood. In the ancient world, this was no small feat as infant mortality was extremely high. Perhaps for the Israelites this was due in part to the fact that women were expected to engage in forced labor while also bearing and raising children—not unlike the expectation placed on Black women who were enslaved in the South.

"The king's logic is not unsound," argues Old Testament scholar Jacqueline Lapsley. She points out the depth of irony found in this part of the story: although both women and men are expected to engage in forced labor, the women are able to not only maintain but increase the number of healthy children they carry to term and raise to adulthood. "In every other case the conditions of hard labor and poverty would tend to a decrease in infant survival rates. But these people, and specifically these women, defy the logic of suffering and death by 'exploding' with children (v. 12)."[14]

Killing them with forced labor didn't work. So Pharaoh decided to try killing the infant sons by asking the midwives to be the ones to do so. We might wonder, Why the midwives? Pharaoh's army could have easily carried out his request. Did he hope to trick the Hebrew people into thinking all these infant deaths were stillbirths? Perhaps a plague or judgment from their God?

Ironically, while Pharaoh thinks men pose a threat to his power, he overlooks the real threat: *God is using the women to set the scene for liberation.* Enslaved to patriarchal ideology, Pharaoh disregards the women's power and character. But Scripture does not. In fact, the narrator of the exodus story shows us how the women begin to act. The story itself reveals with pointed irony the fallacy of the patriarchy, which feeds into the lie that men are more important, more valuable than women. In Pharaoh decreeing twice that the girls shall live (Exod. 1:16, 22), he is intensifying the very power—namely, the women's power—that eventually leads to his undoing.[15]

I've found that God often works this way: shaming power by using those least expected, those whom the world might deem weak or insignificant.

———

In the ancient Near East, midwives typically had two types of tasks. They first performed the physical duties involved in childbirth, which included preparing any necessary equipment and, of course, delivering the child. But midwives played spiritual and healing roles too. In fact, midwifery was often understood as a religious vocation in the ancient world. Not only did a midwife comfort the mother; she prompted "magical" or religious protection over the woman and her infant by performing rituals, like placing ointment on the child and rubbing the child with salt.[16] These were seen as sacred acts. The embodied wisdom of the midwives in Exodus came together with their faith in God to bring forth new life into the world. The text tells us that because the midwives feared God, they didn't do what the king of Egypt had told them to do.

I can't help but notice how often we talk about the midwives in passing: as nothing more than women who disobeyed Pharaoh. But history proves they were more than that. The midwives were ancient keepers of sabiduría, our ancestral abuelitas who carried medicina (medicine) in their hands. And they were women who loved God. Their faith—lived out through their roles as spiritual healers and cocreators, co-madres of new life—prompted them to engage in civil disobedience, to enact justice, not unlike many courageous mujeres throughout history. Shiphrah and Puah were spiritual leaders and healers, akin to curanderas.

In traditional Indigenous culture—as well as many Latine cultures today—curanderas are healers, people who have a spiritual wisdom to cure everyday ailments using food, herbs, and prayers. Curanderas take a holistic approach to wellness, generally believing that disease is caused by social, psychological, physical, environmental, and spiritual factors.

While these traditional forms of healing are often demonized in Western culture, thought of as antithetical to the Christian God, Indigenous and modern-day curanderas were and are very similar to the ancient midwives who were blessed by the same God whom evangelicals claim to worship.

Instead of killing the Hebrew boys as instructed, the midwives let them live—an audacious move. But there's something unique about their plan. In Exodus 1:18, Pharaoh finds out what they're doing and asks them, "Why have you done this? Why have you let the boys live?" (NIV). We are unsure how Pharaoh found out, as the text makes no mention. Was he keeping track? Did a spy inform him? The midwives answer, "Hebrew women are not like Egyptian women; they are *vigorous* and give birth before the midwives arrive" (v. 19 NIV, emphasis mine). However, scholars argue that the word *hayot*, usually translated as "vigorous," "strong," or "lively" in this verse, is softened too much by most translators. Instead, the literal translation is closer to "brutish, animalistic, unrefined."[17]

Hebrew scholar Tikva Frymer-Kensky advocates for "animals" as the proper translation, arguing that midwives would certainly not compliment the Hebrews over the Egyptian women. Instead, building on the fact that Pharaoh sees Israel as other, they make an ethnic slur belittling these so-called others. In this way, they demonstrate to Pharaoh that they are not in favor of the Hebrews, essentially causing him to fall for their trick.[18] Thus, it might be that the midwives are not just disobeying the pharaoh but using his own cultural bias against him,[19] essentially using the tools of empire to deconstruct empire—a common tactic in imperial rhetoric. (In postcolonial theory, *mimicry* refers to the act of taking on the colonizer's politics or attitudes as a form of mockery.)

The courage of the two midwives in defying Pharaoh is motivated by the fact that they fear God more than they fear Pharaoh. The fear of God is associated with courage and sabiduría to act carefully among oppressing powers and to resist them in ways that are not used by those with access to coercive authority.[20] Womanist biblical scholar Renita Weems notes that the midwives' deceit is a conventional weapon of the powerless—especially women in the Hebrew Scriptures—against those in power: "[It is] the weapon of deception where the 'truth' is not defined by the powerful but becomes the priority of the underclass to interpret and shape according to their own reality."[21]

Pharaoh is unsuccessful in his attempt to exterminate God's people because he underestimates the tenacity and creative power of the midwives. The humor in their answer to him is compounded by God's response. Because the midwives fear God and thereby disobey Pharaoh, God rewards them by making them very successful and granting them families of their own. More successful midwives mean that fewer children die at birth, and as a result, Israel grows even more numerous.[22] "They are the mothers of a revolution waged by women," writes womanist scholar Wilda Gafney. "They likely enlisted untold numbers of birthing-women and expectant mothers in their resistance movement."[23]

Ultimately, the midwives' resistance set the stage for others, including Moses's mother, Jochebed. In this way, they acted as "midwives" in more ways than one. They birthed resistance in the other mujeres in the narrative. And so it is the case with our abuelas and what they have passed on to us: their co-madreing, or co-mothering. They help bring forth liberation and healing in our relationships with one another.

We meet Jochebed—Moses, Aaron, and Miriam's mother—in the following chapter. The first thing we learn is that Jochebed is pregnant, a decision that at the time could be perceived as defiant due to Pharaoh's instruction to the people of Egypt to cast every son into the Nile. After giving birth to Moses, Jochebed hides him for three months. Then the text says that "when she couldn't hide him any longer, she took a reed basket and sealed it up with black tar" (Exod. 2:3). Here, Jochebed shows us that she is a madre of embodied wisdom, creating a safe space for her son by the work of her hands—and by the knowledge and gifts she receives from the land.

Her wisdom and the wisdom of the midwives carry ancestral knowledge, medicina, and healing.

Jochebed then put her child in the basket and set the basket among the reeds at the riverbank (Exod. 2:3)—yet another act of civil disobedience in Exodus. Jochebed is an example of a mother who makes bold decisions for her children; her last act in Scripture is securing herself a place as her son's wet nurse once he is discovered. What's interesting is that the text does not mention her husband or whether her husband was present in Jochebed's decision to put her child in the river.

Here we find another ironic twist to the story: Pharaoh's means of killing—the Nile—became the means of Moses's deliverance, thanks to his mother.

"For people whose survival depended on the inscrutable moods of the Tigris, Euphrates, and Nile, water represented both life and death. . . . Rivers brimmed with fickle possibility."[24] Through the sacred water flowing within the Nile, liberation was birthed in a people.

And it was in this water where Pharaoh's daughter entered to bathe herself (Exod. 2:5)—where she found the baby Moses protected by the plants of the earth.

Pharaoh's daughter is a poignant character for many of us who find ourselves in privileged spaces. While she isn't named in the Hebrew Bible, parts of Jewish tradition have given her the name Bithiah, which means "daughter of God."[25] Bithiah grew up in her father's palace as a child of Egyptian greatness. However, she didn't allow her privilege to cause her to ignore injustice— particularly injustices brought on by her own father. Her compassion led her to deceive her father in order to let the child, Moses, live. When given the opportunity, she chose to resist, to do what was right, taking on the role of a co-madre, co-mother, of Moses.

As women in a hierarchical, male-led society,[26] the women in Exodus understood what it meant to be othered; however, as mujeres who feared God instead of the powers at hand, they made audacious, courageous, and bold decisions.

What's fascinating about this narrative (and many others in Scripture) is how God blesses their civil disobedience and acts of deceit. It might sound shocking, as it feels so contrary to what modern evangelicalism teaches a "God-fearer" to do. Their disobedience of the king awards them divine favor; the text says, "And because the midwives respected God, God gave them households of their own" (Exod. 1:21). This is yet another reminder of how nuanced faith is, how God meets God's people in the complex reality of what it means to "do right" or "live justly." Through their defiance, their stories become stories of abuelita resistance and abuelita survival that secure the future of their familias. But more than that, their stories are stories of embodied wisdom, creativity, and even art making that bring forth healing and justice.

Their stories are also scandalous, stories that aren't traditionally told or celebrated in a culture that has domesticated Scripture and what it means to follow Jesus in a world in which patriarchy and whiteness rule. I wonder what our churches would look like if we celebrated and emulated the faith and the knowledge of overlooked women whom God used to liberate entire peoples and challenge entire empires.

Through the behind-the-scenes, subversive work of their hands, the midwives teach us that the lowliest in society can bring about the most change, that they can be agents of healing, and that liberation is the heartbeat of God.

This reminds me of the mujer who finds Jesus sitting at the water well (John 4). In the narrative, Jesus asks the Samaritan woman for a drink as she approaches the well with her water jug. I love her response, as she challenges Jesus: "Why do you, a Jewish man, ask for something to drink from me, a Samaritan woman?" (v. 9).

Jesus doesn't just talk to an otherwise despised woman—as many theologians have pointed out to be radical—but he assumes her agency and engages her in mutuality. Jesus welcomes the Samaritan woman's challenge, participating with her in teología en conjunto, the act of theologizing together, in collaboration.[27] And through their back-and-forth exchange, the mujer at the well encounters the Living Water—our sacred water who himself heals, gives life, and restores. The mujer immediately runs back to her community to deliver the message.

Like many of the women in Cuba, the Black women in the South, or the Hebrew women in Egypt, the mujer at the well collaborates with God to seek the liberation of her people. And like the story of both Israel's and my familia's exodus, it began with a trip to the water.

5

Telling La Verdad

Every Saturday night was domino night at Abuela's house.

And that's certainly not a passing detail. Domino night at Abuela's was serious—the climax of our week. About twenty members of our familia would huddle in her small duplex, the adults taking turns playing a two-on-two domino tournament that had been going on for several decades, since Cuba. As kids, my primos and primas (cousins), my siblings, and I looked forward to Saturday night every single week: no bedtime and watching episodes of *Sábado Gigante*, the longest-running variety show in television history—a three-hour, one-stop entertainment show that was a combination of *Maury*, *The Price Is Right*, and *American Idol*—made specifically for Latines.[1] During commercials, my cousin Yetzabel and I would put on Abuela's dresses, stuff pillows underneath them, decorate our eyelids bright blue and our lips bright red, and put on a play for the adults, yelling in Spanglish like two loud and passionate tías—our mannerisms and phrases picked up from our familia's day-to-day conversations. On most Saturdays the children would be asleep before the adults. We'd pass out all over the house, sweaty and exhausted from playing until way too late, often waking up to the sound of our parents and grandparents yelling at each other after a bad move or a lost game.

"¡Por qué tiraste esa ficha!" (Why did you use that domino!)

"¡Te gané con la misma ficha tuya!" (I beat you with your own domino!)

It wasn't uncommon for their games to last until the sun came up, the earliest nights usually ending around three in the morning. This happened every single weekend for nearly the first two decades of my life. It was playful, but oh, it was serious. Nietzsche said that a person's maturity comes in regaining the seriousness that they had lost as a child at play. I think Cubans embody this well, most particularly with their dominoes.

There's a famous street in the heart of Little Havana in Miami called Calle Ocho. Many tourists make this a stop on their Miami tour to soak in the smell of Cuban cigars, the sound of salsa on the street, and the famous Domino Park, where dozens of Cubans gather around tables all day, each and every day of the week, to catch a few games. And it never fails—each time you pass by, you'll catch a glimpse of a heated debate about why a person decided to use a specific ficha (domino). Chances are these same abuelos, abuelas, tíos, and tías have been huddled around these same tables for years. The polka-dot ivory tiles offer both a distraction and a comfort, a reminder of a familiar time. Seeing these comrades huddled around una mesa—whether familia or not—you'd assume that dominoes bonded them, gave them an excuse to get close, so close that exchanging heated words over a bad move would be no big deal. But the truth is, exile brought them together. The small polka-dot tile simply gave them an excuse to just be, to exist together as a community with a shared history, a shared trauma.

Those domino tables were life lessons in my familia: we speak (or yell) the truth no matter what. I learned very young that when there's a problem, you confront it. It's how you get by. It's how you show up week after week and sit across from the same partner you've had for decades and trust they won't let you down by putting the wrong ficha on the table. And if they let you down? You tell them how you feel. For me, confrontation has always been equated with intimacy. These lessons pump through my veins as powerfully as a cafecito at three in the afternoon. It wasn't until I left my context, my culture, that I realized how rare it is to value confrontation and truth telling, and what lengths many people will go to in order to silence the prophets in our midst.

⚯

I imagine Huldah the prophet held to similar values.

Her story is found in 2 Kings 22 and 2 Chronicles 34. It's not surprising that we don't know much about her or hear of her often. I wonder if her story goes untold because it's hard to reconcile a truth-telling woman, a prophet who instructs a man—the king—in the way of God, with the narratives that are forced on women by much of the church. Some in the church tell women that they can't lead men, that the Bible says so, but what about Huldah? She was called by God to tell the truth. If I would have known her story years earlier, perhaps I wouldn't have spent so much time doubting myself, my upbringing, or even my culture when I was introduced to white evangelicalism.

I wish we knew more about Huldah's calling. We know about other prophets and how they were called by God to do the seemingly impossible work of telling people to get their acts together. But Huldah? What was it like for a woman to be called to such a powerful position of spiritual leadership and authority? Did she have a vision that empowered her like Isaiah did, or was she terrified and trying to get out of it like Jonah? I wonder if she was young like Josiah, who became king as a child and eventually went to Huldah for spiritual counsel. Were there women in her life, abuelitas who discipled her, told her about her antepasados and everything they went through in Egypt, in the desert? Did she have role models like Miriam, a woman without husband or children, the first woman to ever be called a prophet? Did Huldah look up to the way Miriam led Israel in song and dance and to how they were committed to her—refusing to march in the wilderness until she was healed from her disease (Num. 12:15)?

While we don't know Huldah's background, Scripture does fill us in on her role when the book of the law was discovered by Hilkiah the high priest during King Josiah's reign. After finding out that God was angry with the nation of Judah because their ancestors disobeyed the words of the law, Josiah instructed the high priest along with the royal court to go to Huldah and "ask the LORD" to receive direction from God through the prophet (2 Kings 22:13; 2 Chron. 34:21).

And Huldah did just that—boldly. She warned of the coming destruction, declaring that the written word they found was indeed God's true word. She also delivered good news, validating Josiah's repentance on first reading the book. She let the messengers know that Josiah's actions would bring forth peace. After Huldah's word got back to him, Josiah responded by continuing his reform.

Huldah's prophetic words shifted national policy. Her commitment to telling God's truth—even and especially the hard truth—specifically to men in power, changed the course of history.

———

At around age six, I came home from school with my stomach in knots because I had just heard from a classmate that Santa does not exist. As soon as I walked through the door, I sat Abuela and Mom down on the couch next to me.

"We need to talk," I said, while my legs dangled from the side of the couch.

"¿Que te pasa?" (What's wrong?) asked Abuela.

"Is it true that there's no such thing as Santa?" I asked with a straight, serious face.

"Where'd you hear that?" asked Mom.

"At school."

"Es verdad. No hay Santa Claus" (It's true. There's no Santa Claus), confessed Abuela.

I burst into a fit of tears. Abuela and Mom went in for a hug, but I pushed them away with as much force as my tiny body could muster.

They both tried to reassure me with "lo siento" (I'm sorry), but I just couldn't be consoled. It was earth shattering.

"I'm not crying because there's no Santa; I'm crying because you lied to me!" I told them.

They looked at each other rather amused, trying to hold in smiles.

"You're right," Mom said. "We promise we won't lie to you again."

I still hold them to this promise, because for me, to be Cuban is to be a truth teller. That's part of our survival. Papi's commitment to his truth led him to board a small boat in the middle of a treacherous night, unsure of what was lurking underneath the water.

I come from a legacy and a community of people committed to their truth. This applies to the thousands of people who find themselves on borders, who might have fled their homes in an attempt to forge a better future for their familias.

Oftentimes we tell the truth most powerfully by our actions, with our bodies, our lived experiences bearing the scars of honesty. Abuela bears those scars still today; her fading memory is a treasure box that contains these gems. Memory is an interesting thing.

~

When I began telling the truth about my experiences with racism and sexism in the church, I was quickly labeled "divisive." However, I always wonder why folks are so quick to think that speaking out against things like sexism, racism, abuse, homophobia, ableism, and such is more divisive than actually being sexist, racist, abusive, homophobic, or ableist. Speaking out against injustice isn't what divides—instead, acting in ways that are divisive does.

Whenever I hear the word *divisive* used to keep others silent from speaking up against injustice, I'm reminded of God's words spoken through the prophet Jeremiah: "They dress the wound of my people as though it were not serious. 'Peace, peace,' they say, when there is no peace" (Jer. 6:14 NIV).

True peace is birthed when injustice is unearthed, excavated, laid bare, exposed. Ephesians 5:9–11 attests to this when it says, "Light produces fruit that consists of every sort of goodness, justice, and truth. Therefore, test everything to see what's pleasing to the Lord, and don't participate in the unfruitful actions of darkness. Instead, you should reveal the truth about them." Thus, telling the truth is not an act of division but a brave pursuit of what's good and just.

This is why telling the truth is an act of resistance, and for me, truth telling was born at the domino table with a room full of playful and angry Cubans yelling over who placed the right ficha or made the wrong move. What I love about two-on-two domino games is that you cannot win if you're not paying extra-close attention to what your partner is doing. Experts in the game are able to count what numbers are on the table and guess, based on what numbers people play, which fichas are left. As a kid, I was always so fascinated by how the adults did that so well. I'd sit on my padrino's (godfather's) lap amazed at how he knew exactly what fichas his partner had without ever looking at them. Perhaps this is why they got so angry when their partner placed an unexpected ficha on the table; it was a betrayal of the commitment they had made to each other when the game began. They were in it together, and they knew every move they'd make. They'd study and memorize their partners like professional dancers attempting to nail a new routine. They memorized each move of the hand, the looks from the table, the confidence their partners would give off when they had a good hand.

I often wonder what kind of world this would be if we committed to knowing each other, to belonging to one another, the way my familia did with their domino partners. Because the fact is, our fight for an equitable future is intimately connected to our belongingness with one another. As one of our well-known madrinas Mother Teresa once said, "If we have no peace, it is because we have forgotten that we belong to each other."[2]

I think this is foundational to an abuelita faith: recognizing the sacred belonging we have to Creator and every created thing. But we cannot belong to one another if we're not committed to telling the truth about ourselves and each other. Injustice affects both the oppressor and the oppressed, so we must tell the truth about the past—and the ways we have disrupted our sacred belongingness—so we may heal our future.

Zora Neale Hurston says, "If you're silent about your pain, they'll kill you and say you enjoyed it"[3]—a powerful statement that bears theological weight when it comes to the story of Hannah in 1 Samuel 1 and 2. You may have heard Hannah often described as the poor helpless wife whose husband loved her despite her inability to conceive.

In 1 Samuel 1, Hannah is distraught not only because she cannot have children but because her husband's other wife, Peninnah, mocks her consistently for her barrenness. The story highlights the fact that this would happen every year when they went to the temple in Shiloh to make their sacrifices. Every year, Hannah would be reminded of her pain and would spend the trip in tears, unable to eat. In the story, she's so distraught that she goes to the temple by herself to present herself before God (1 Sam. 1:9). That's where she is met by the high priest, Eli, who accuses her of being drunk. She tells Eli she isn't drunk, and she makes a promise to God that if God gives her a son, then she'll devote him to God as a Nazirite.[4] Hannah eventually gives birth to Samuel—a prophet and priest who will end up changing the course of Israel's history.

Most traditional readings of Hannah portray her as helpless, a victim who's taunted and even jealous—a common portrayal of women in the Hebrew Scriptures. Her husband, Elkanah, is often praised as the loving husband who loves her in a way that is unique for men during his time—over and above his other wife, Peninnah, who had given him several children.

But there is more to her story than her being a victim or her husband being the one primarily worthy of praise. Hannah speaks her truth, and she speaks it boldly, not only to Eli but in a subversive poem that Mary's own Magnificat is believed to be modeled after (Luke 1:46–55).

—⁓⁓—

There is power in naming. Many communities throughout history have considered naming a sacred process. This is true not only for a myriad of cultures across times and places but for God's people in Scripture. Because Israelite women represent only 8 percent of attested Israelite personal names,[5] Hannah's name—mentioned fourteen times within two chapters—stands out within the story. Not only is she named more often than her husband and Eli the priest, but her name appears almost as many times as the matriarchs Sarah, Rebekah, Rachel, and Leah.

Additionally, the narrator often depicts Hannah as the subject rather than the object of the Hebrew verbs in the story. This is something that is not particularly common when it comes to women in the Hebrew Bible. In this same way, we notice that Hannah speaks more than she is addressed in her narrative. These details alone should cause us to pause, to turn our attention to the insight we might learn from this overlooked, albeit important, abuelita theologian.

As we know from other narratives in the Bible, barrenness was—and still is—a big deal for many families, a potential point of pain for mothers and fathers alike. While having children was a burden for men, who needed to provide for every member in their household, women usually bore the greatest burden in ancient Israel. Hannah most likely grew up hearing that in order to be a good wife, she must be able to produce children. In Jewish custom, a man could divorce his wife if she did not have children after ten years, a detail that probably added to Hannah's anxiety.[6]

Hannah's relationship to Peninnah has been compared to that of Sarah to Hagar—another story that addresses similar themes of rivalry and barrenness. But a few notable details set Hannah apart. For example, in Sarah's story it is her husband, Abraham, who receives the revelation of their future child and is involved in naming him. Hannah, however, takes the lead in her story. She not only prays for and dedicates her son to God but also names him, participating in the social authority of making decisions about the future of her child.

She is cocreator, a co-madre in Israel's future.

As the narrative unfolds, I can't help but notice the ways Hannah is othered by the three individuals whom she interacts with. The first is, of course, the "rival wife," Peninnah, but the same is true for two unexpected characters: her husband and Eli the priest. Their conversations are key to the story.

Hannah's distress is particularly acute during the family's annual trek to Shiloh, where Elkanah's differential allotment of the sacrificial portions is on full display.[7] Hannah receives only one portion because she is only one individual, which causes her to weep and leaves her unable to partake in the sacrificial feast.[8] Mirroring the narrative of Sarah and Hagar, Peninnah torments Hannah, and Elkanah responds by asking Hannah why she's crying. Elkanah is often portrayed in a positive light, as someone who cares about his wife by taking notice of her, but looking deeper, I wonder if he does more harm, if he exacerbates disharmony in his family with his words. "Why won't you eat? Why are you so sad?" he asks in 1 Samuel 1:8.

Does Elkanah not know his wife? Hasn't he seen her pain or heard her struggle? How can he not know why she is sad or why she won't eat? In his questions it seems he doesn't allow space for Hannah to answer. This makes me wonder if they were rhetorical questions that only silenced his suffering wife further.[9]

When Hannah doesn't respond, he treats her sorrow as if it's about him: "Aren't I worth more to you than ten sons?" (1 Sam. 1:8). Some argue that Elkanah decides for his wife that his closeness is more important to her than her own children would be. Who is he to make that call, to make her pain about him—especially considering the economic vulnerability a woman without sons would find herself in if her husband were to die? It's also interesting that Elkanah "consoles" his wife by claiming his love for her, but not her love for him. Is he diminishing Hannah's suffering by attempting to show that it is unjustified?[10] "Elkanah is therefore guilty not only of insensitivity to his wife's feelings," notes Israeli biblical scholar Yairah Amit, "but also of disregard for her future."[11] I wonder how different the story might have turned out if Hannah's husband would have listened to understand his wife, honored her without being unfair with his words or further causing her marginalization.

Perhaps Elkanah was doing the best he knew how, and while he might have been well intentioned, it doesn't change the outcome. It's the impact that matters. This is particularly poignant considering that the text says that Elkanah loved Hannah, presumably more than Penninah, which is why he would give her double portions (1 Sam. 1:5).

Hannah doesn't seem to feel any better after her conversation with her husband. She then takes her anguish to God and begins to pray by the temple where Eli, the high priest, is seated.

While her conversation with her husband was problematic, her conversation with the high priest is worse. As Hannah is praying, Eli observes her mouth, and before even taking a moment to speak with her, he judges her: "How long are you going to stay drunk? Put away your wine" (1 Sam. 1:14 NIV). Eli, the high priest, jumps to unfounded conclusions with insufficient evidence and labels her a drunk. This unjust criticism further marginalizes Hannah, particularly because of his position of authority.[12]

This exchange in Scripture has been a source of comfort for me, a reminder that men in power—those with "spiritual authority" like Eli—can be responsible for dismissing, judging, or assuming the worst of us. This story tells me I'm not alone, that this tale is as old as time.

I met a group of young women in one of the first churches I attended during my early years in seminary. After connecting with them several times, I suggested getting together regularly for a Bible study. I was looking to engage with younger women to discuss life, God, and such in community—an opportunity to perhaps develop a mentor or discipleship relationship with them if they desired it. They seemed excited, so we began getting together once a week at each other's houses to pray, chat about Scripture, eat, and spend time together.

After a few weeks, the pastor of this church caught wind of our small group time and began asking questions, wondering about my motives. He even asked my spouse (who I was still dating at the time), Taylor, to meet. During their time together, the pastor interrogated Taylor about me, my background, and my upbringing and asked him bluntly what my sins were. Taylor and I didn't have the language or the understanding back then to recognize this red flag or other signs of spiritual abuse (which later became clear), but we felt there was something off-putting and inappropriate about the situation and particularly his questions. It wasn't too long before the pastor began telling people in the congregation (who he didn't know were my friends) that I was unsubmissive—difficult and problematic—because I didn't *ask him for permission* to befriend young women in the church. Like many who abuse their authority, this pastor seemed to prefer control over his congregation to his congregation's spiritual health or growth.

Before having a conversation with me, the pastor labeled me "suspect." He questioned my motives and began spewing rumors about me not being submissive to his authority and thus to God's. Taylor and I eventually met with him and then left the church, but not before countless sleepless nights. For weeks I wept, questioning my relationship with God, wondering what in the world I did wrong to make a pastor speak ill of me behind my back, to assume the worst of me before having a conversation with me or getting to know me. I now know that this pastor's actions and words were rooted in sin, patriarchy, and spiritual abuse, but I didn't recognize this back then. I suffered for months and felt like a bad Christian, person, woman. When someone with supposed authority, especially "spiritual" authority, makes you feel this way, it can feel unbearable and make you question whether everything about you is wrong, evil, against God. Thankfully, after countless prayers and conversations with trusted pastors and other members of the congregation, I was able to find that inkling of trust in God and in myself to pull out of my grief and leave that church. This is part of what sparked my leaving the denomination entirely.

It's not uncommon for men—particularly men from the dominating culture who are used to being in power—to use their so-called authority and their own interpretations of Scripture to silence us, to keep us in what they think is "our place." Thinking about that time of my life still pains me, but Hannah's boldness energizes me.

After her encounter with her husband, Hannah seeks God in prayer. She confidently asks God to look at her, to notice her, particularly when others, like her own husband, don't see who she is.[13] By coming to God and asking that God would remember her, Hannah shifts her identity away from being a wife or a barren woman, and she proclaims her truth. Hannah asserts herself as a beloved child of God—a powerful and bold proclamation of belonging, one that I think many of our abuelitas know and live by.

In 2016 a prominent right-wing public voice got into an exchange on Twitter with Rachel Held Evans over abortion. He called her a heretic and a blasphemer, to which she responded, "That is a lie. I am a beloved child of God, . . . and nothing you say can take that away from [me]."[14] These powerful prophetic words have stayed with me. One of the boldest declarations we can make is that we are beloved mijas and mijos, children of God, no matter what anyone says. I think Hannah understood this, and I think her story bears so much weight because of it, especially in her encounter with Eli.

After she's accused by Eli of being a drunk, Hannah takes that energy of being a beloved of God and speaks—declares—her truth boldly yet again. "Not so," she replies to the high priest, "I am a woman deeply troubled" (1 Sam. 1:15 NIV). Lillian Klein explains that in the structure of Hannah's response, she almost literally centers her words on the most significant aspect of her visit to the temple—namely, that she's been pouring out her soul before God.[15]

It's interesting to note that both of the men Hannah interacts with in the story (her husband and the high priest) are "righteous" and admirable, but "they're both so involved with their own perceptions that they fail to comprehend a suffering woman, a woman who is wife to the first and a devotee of the temple of God to the second."[16] Hannah is marginalized by both of these men, but in her speaking her truth and declaring her worth to both God and the high priest, Hannah evolves into a paradigm, a model woman.[17]

Hannah's story culminates in her second prayer, her poem in 1 Samuel 2. In fact, it's the only poetic passage in all of 1 Samuel, which not only distinguishes her in the narrative but, I believe, awards her the title *theologian*. Hannah's first prayer focuses on her own need, on her anguish, and her status before God. But her second prayer? It is a bold declaration of justice, a prayer focused on the oppressed:

> God raises the poor from the dust,
>> lifts up the needy from the garbage pile.
> God sits them with officials,
>> gives them the seat of honor! (v. 8)

Telling the truth is a catalyst for healing, not just for ourselves but for those in our communities—the marginalized, the oppressed—and those who come after us, our children and their children. Some Indigenous teachers have taught that when you heal, you do so seven generations forward. Some include seven generations in the past too.

As other madrinas in the faith have said, "La verdad trae justicia." (Truth brings justice.)[18] Truth telling heals us and testifies to our sacred belonging—with its end goal in justice.

Remembering is a central theme in the story of Israel. In Scripture, God is consistently urging God's people to remember where they've come from, what they've been through, whose they are, and ultimately, who God is. In Exodus 23:9, God calls God's people to remember how they were oppressed so that they don't oppress. Postcolonial writers and critics emphasize the temptation for oppressed people to turn around and do to others what empire did to them. "No matter our station in life, we all may at any time find ourselves in a position to exploit or oppress another person," notes womanist biblical scholar Mitzi Smith. "We all have potential victims. And we can be passive participants in our own exploitation."[19]

Just like the Israelites were prone to forget, so my own people often perpetuate the oppressor narrative. Oppressed people often adopt cultural biases about themselves—the racial patterns and attitudes that have been inherited, especially those of fear and prejudice. As Gloria Anzaldúa points out, it's easier to repeat than to resist them, passing on to children and friends the oppressor's ideologies.[20]

Many Cubans who were welcomed with open arms to the US have decided to meet others who are fleeing political unrest (like they once were) with crossed arms, failing to remember how they needed justice—mercy, love, and compassion—at a crucial point in their lives.

We are a people that remembers, but we are also a people that forgets.

Perhaps this is the lure of power, what whiteness convinces many people of color to believe: that assimilation equates providence, comfort, ease. To this end, Mexican American writer Antonio De Loera-Brust explains that non-Black Latino communities in the US too often embrace the country's anti-Black attitudes, stereotypes, and worldviews as part of a process of assimilation. "This is a well-beaten path in US immigrant history," he says. "Many immigrant groups have sensed in anti-Blackness an opportunity to assimilate into whiteness, or at least move into closer proximity with it."[21] All across Latine societies is a worshiping of whiteness that has been around for centuries, since colonizers deemed those with darker skin as "savage," "uncivilized," "dangerous."

Being a truth teller means that I must fight anti-Blackness in my own community and that I must look backward and tell the truth about our collective past and our sacred belonging. I must remember and aim to lead my people in remembrance for the liberation and healing of us all—generations in the past and future.

6

Cosiendo and Creating

Hosting domino night wasn't something Abuela had to do; it was something she *got* to do—every single weekend—for decades. Her house was the epicenter of activity. The front door was constantly swinging open with friends and family gathering together for un juego (a game), a cafecito, or dinner, oftentimes all three. But it wasn't just dominoes and dinners that constantly filled Abuela's house with people.

When she first arrived from Cuba, Abuela worked in a clothing factory. She was among the tens of thousands of Cuban women who found jobs in manufacturing when they arrived in Miami. Many of them, like Abuela, were experienced at cosiendo (sewing and pattern making). In fact, Miami's golden era of fashion can be attributed to that time in history when Cuban women brought their cheap labor and their invaluable skills. Miami's fashion industry is built on the backs of Latinas, Abuela's included.

Years later, Abuela was able to create her own designs like she did in Cuba and start her own small business selling clothes from her home. To me, Abuela was like a magician or a fairy godmother, creating entire worlds out of nothing, beauty from scraps. She would spend hours sketching designs. I was always in awe of how they seamlessly came to life.

Every Halloween, Abuela would spend weeks creating the most magical costumes for me. I'd stand on a small stool in front of the mirror, twirling around in circles while she carefully joined pieces of fabric, holding them together with needles that every so often would poke my skin. "Cuidado, no te muevas tanto" (Be careful, don't move so much), she'd tell me through pinched lips, holding a needle in her mouth to free up her hands.

My very own universe was being created with each fitting.

For several years, we'd enter costume competitions at our local mall. One notable year, I got on stage with my Disney princess costume and danced my heart out to la "Macarena," shaking my hips like Shakira. I won first place that night and felt like a million bucks, beaming with pride as I showed off the outfit Abuela made for me.

We'd regularly visit the local fabric store at the strip mall down the street and spend hours lost in the sea of colors. Abuela was friends with the ladies who worked there, and together we'd dream up outfits. They'd stand me on the large cutting table and hold different fabrics to my body, imagining how the material might drape over me as a dress. The silk and satin felt like liquid cream on my skin. They'd compliment me as they wrapped me in cloth: "¡Ay, mira que linda!" (Oh, look how how pretty!) And my cheeks would burn hot, blush bright red. It was an embodied experience; most of my senses were engaged.

The sound of Abuela's olive green sewing machine became a lullaby. I often fell asleep to the repetitive *chukka chukka chukka* as the needle punched through the fabric.

I loved learning from Abuela and would spend hours watching her. I was so proud when she taught me how to lick a thread and get it through the hole of a needle. How did she have such precision? Such patience? How did her hands wield so much knowledge, create so much life?

———

Tejana poet Carolina Hinojosa-Cisneros writes, "I believe our hands complicate time. If we're lucky enough, they help carry on the stories of our antepasados. This is why we write, knit, compose, cook, and so much more, We are all each a sacred text."[1]

Sewing, stitching, and weaving traditional textiles is an ancient craft that has been passed down by our ancestors. Indigenous women across time have sewed and traded clothes and other materials in their communities, making the textile industry one of the earliest industries known to humankind.[2] Throughout history, Indigenous people have used Creator's gifts of the land for many things: from protection, to keeping warm, to decorating their bodies for ceremonial reasons. For the Aymara—the Indigenous people of Bolivia—sacred weavings are expressions of their philosophy and the basis for their social organization.[3] In native African communities, garments are worn to mark a special ritual or passage of time as people move from one spiritual or life stage to another.[4]

The art of making or creating has always been more than just a physical craft; it has served spiritual purposes as well.

With cosiendo, both the mind and the hands think and design. It's an embodied experience that involves the spiritual disciplines of remaining focused, present, and engaged. Creating with our hands also involves the art of remembering. It is a way that we tell stories about ourselves and our communities. This process invites the artist to take an inward journey "moving the body to rhythms of the earth."[5] This sacred activity is one of cocreation, of connecting to the divine through the earth's gifts that are given to us; it is an intrinsic form of spiritual knowledge that is carried from generation to generation.

To this day, I'll visit Abuela wearing a new article of clothing bought in the store. She'll stare at the fabric, run her fingers over the buttons, and inspect the hems as if she were examining a foreign object. Even though Abuela can no longer sew, her mind never forgets. She'll often hold the article of clothing between her fingers and rub gently as she asks me where I bought it. When I mention the store, she'll respond, "Ay, no hacen cosas de la misma manera que antes" (They don't make things the same way they did before). I'll nod in agreement; the fast fashion from which we fill our closets has lost the spirituality—the sacred and embodied wisdom and love—that was once used to create it.

In many ways, capitalism has destroyed the sacred art of cocreation through art making by turning the fashion industry into an element of global injustice, exacerbating the hellish conditions of garment workers across the world. In 2013 over a thousand factory workers were killed in the Rana Plaza building in Bangladesh because of deadly working conditions. Only five months earlier, over a hundred other workers died in another tragic accident on the outskirts of Dhaka.[6] Thousands of people in communities across the globe die every year for similar reasons, including children. Child labor—often considered a modern form of slavery—is a common injustice perpetuated by the fast-fashion industry.[7]

Additionally, discarding clothes has become one of the fastest growing categories of waste in the world, with hundreds of thousands of tons of clothes sent to landfills every year.[8] I believe the groans of the earth and our ancestors call out the injustices that are birthed as we get further away from art making as a spiritual endeavor, as an act of healing, mending, and creating. I feel this through Abuela's deep sighs when her leathery fingers graze my clothes. What once adorned my body through the love and care of her hands, has now turned into the stench of injustice and death.

In the 1970s, a violent US-backed coup led by General Augusto Pinochet ousted Chile's first democratically elected socialist president, Salvador Allende. Four years later, Pinochet and his military regime officially came into power. The Nixon administration set the scene for Pinochet's repressive dictatorship, which was involved in systemic and widespread human rights abuses.[9] During his vicious regime, tens of thousands of Chileans were shot, imprisoned, and tortured to death.[10] Over three thousand were kidnapped or vanished without a trace. While it was the military's desire for these abuses to be forgotten, ignored, or erased, a group of madrinas, mamás, and abuelitas decided to make sure that wasn't the case by turning their skill of art making into resistance.

The women in this group were known as arpilleristas, a name given to a group—usually of women—that creates arpilleras, artwork that is typically embroidered on the back of sackcloth. Many of them were mothers and grandmothers of the kidnapped, and they came together to sew political images and protest the loss of their loved ones. Their quilts were stitched with faces of young activists and with signs that read, "¿Dónde están los desaparecidos?" (Where are the disappeared?) They also sewed radical images of military persons arresting and torturing innocent people. Eventually, the arpilleristas began using the clothing and even the hair of the deceased.

Chilean American writer Marjorie Agosín talks about the power of the human hand: "We live in such a global world where everything is manufactured through machinery," she says, "but by the human hand, [they] constructed [a] story, stitching piece by piece, a life—but not an ordinary life—a life that has been cut off."[11] She explains that their art and their lives became inseparable, and their sewing and stitching became an act of resistance, a way for them to tell their stories. In the fear of this regime, which caused deafening silence, censorship, victimization, and fear in the lives of innocent citizens, these arpilleristas found and used their voice through their craft.

The arpilleristas were subversive in many ways. The fact that they made sewing an act of subversion is subversive in and of itself. Their use of a mundane activity often done in the home—a space to which women were often relegated—made arpillera making highly disruptive, an act of dissent, particularly because they broke from the format of creating traditional art and images to depicting images with overtly political messages. This form of resistance enacted justice as it raised awareness. These women used their skills, their art making, and their cocreation with the elements of the earth to bring about a more just society.

Inés Velásquez-McBryde, a Nicaraguan pastor and a friend of mine, once shared with me the creative ways the abuelitas in her family used the work of their hands. Her abuela, Sara, lived in the mining town of Bonanza, Nicaragua. To give Inés's dad and aunts a chance at a better education, Abuela Sara sent them by train to live with her sister in the capital city of Managua. "Both my tía Zela and my dad would tell me stories about what a costly sacrifice it was emotionally, spiritually, and financially to be 530 kilometers and a ten-hour train ride through treacherous mountains away from family," explains Inés.[12]

Abuela Sara often would mail care packages to send love to her children. As a seamstress, she would include dresses sewn by hand for her daughters in those care packages. With her creative innovation, Abuela Sara would include a letter in the package with coded language to the eldest of the three: "Zela, check the seams in this dress I made for you to see if the length is good. I hope you like it, but do let me know if it fits you well."[13] In the hem were hidden a few rolled-up córdoba bills.

Abuela Sara was not financially rich, but those bills were enough for her children to treat themselves to a little something fun at the pulpería (corner store). Both the handmade gifts and the hard-earned money were the signs of a woman sacrificing and using the work of her hands to provide for and empower the next generation.

Women have been providing and empowering since the beginning, even within the early church. How often have we heard in evangelical circles that men are to be the providers? As I reflect on the mujeres in my own life who worked and provided for their familias, alongside the mujeres in the Bible who did the same for theirs, I can't help but boldly challenge that notion.

For example, all four Gospels show that Jesus accepted women as traveling disciples. In fact, he is arguably one of the few leaders of his day who did so. Luke 8:1–3 describes women disciples like Mary Magdalene, Joanna, Susanna, and "many others," who not only traveled with Jesus but supported him financially out of their own resources.

Joanna is one of the more interesting characters in the Bible because there is so much speculation about who she was. She is understood as the wife of the steward of Herod of Antipas, a woman who apparently traveled on her own or with friends (including Jesus) without fear of reprisal. This is a surprising detail, considering women in early Jewish culture were not supposed to fraternize with men they were not related to, much less travel around Galilee with them.[14] On top of following Jesus around, the Bible says she also supported him financially.

What makes this particularly surprising is the fact that her husband worked for the oppressive tetrarch who beheaded John the Baptist. I wonder, How did Herod feel about his estate manager's wife supporting Jesus? Perhaps the fact that Joanna would leave her home and put her husband's career at risk to follow Jesus shows how attractive his ministry must have been to women. Jesus not only empowered women but brought about a more just society by throwing social norms out the window, and many aspects of the early church reflect this reality.

Mujeres carry medicina in their hands, their hearts, their minds, and their bodies. Throughout the centuries, the weaving of arts has served as a metaphor for healing, showing us how doing so helps to compose and better understand our world. Abuela sewed to heal the wounds of Papi's death. After he died, certain men in the family fought to push Abuela out of the family business in order to gain more money for themselves. In a subversive sense, Abuela used cosiendo to provide economic stability when the pangs of patriarchy and sexism tried to keep her down. Like many women throughout history, Abuela used her craft to mend, restore, and provide. "Art heals our wounded or just plain tired spirits. Art restores our psyche, our spirits, and our bodies to a balanced state of being."[15]

For many of our abuelitas, part of this creative healing includes stitching their stories and lives into offerings of love. Whether for the arpilleristas or our Indigenous ancestors, sewing and stitching has always required attention to the details of the world, including to ourselves and others. This is also true for Abuela. She engaged in her skill as an act of love—to make those in her community feel known, seen. And oh, how we felt these things. Abuela knew how to manipulate the fabric across every curve of our bodies. She knew our measurements, how to make something fit just right.

In Genesis 3, after God has a chat with Eve and Adam about eating the forbidden fruit, the narrator tells us that God made leather clothes and dressed them (Gen. 3:21). I'm struck by how this detail made it into the story—and how familiar it feels. Adam and Eve had already attempted to make clothes to cover their nakedness (3:7), and I imagine their effort was similar to mine as a little girl, when I made my best attempt to pin pieces of clothing together like Abuela, ignorant of how she did it. As my caretaker and provider, Abuela always came along with the right fabric, precision, and intentionality. Even in moments when I may have hurt, angered, or disappointed her in my youth, she always took care of me—like God did Adam and Eve in the garden.

God is a God who creates so much from so little; who is patient and attentive to the smallest details; who knows every crevice of our bodies and seeks to care, clothe, provide, and empower us; and whose focus is the flourishing of humans.

If mujeres are made in God's image, then we, too, carry these same things inside our bodies: we are cocreators, healers, and providers. The act of giving love through the art made with our hands is an act of deep healing power, and we see this through the myriad of women in the Bible and throughout history who have sewn as a way to enact justice.

For Abuela, it was also a means for her own liberation—it was a way for her to challenge gender roles by contributing to the well-being of the household through selling items.[16]

⸻

Tabitha is another New Testament character who carried medicina in her hands. While her story is often lost within Peter's, taking a closer look allows us to find several nuggets of wisdom that speak to an abuelita faith.

Tabitha was a Jewish woman living in Joppa, which was located on the border between an area that was predominantly Jewish and an area that was predominantly gentile. Locating a person, whether a character in Scripture or someone interpreting that character, is of primary importance. As womanist scholar Febbie Dickerson says, "Her [Tabitha's] situatedness impacts her story, and that context must be respected."[17] I love this insight because it's not only true for Tabitha but for every single one of us.

The text also offers an interesting detail: despite her Jewish identity, Scripture lets us know that Tabitha also has a Greek name, Dorcas, as she is living in Roman territory. In Acts 9:40 Peter calls her by her Aramaic name, not her Greek one. This can be understood as a decolonizing narrative device, as she is marked by her precolonial name.[18]

Tabitha stands out to me, not just as a woman who provided like Joanna but as one who did so by cosiendo. She is introduced in Acts 9:36 as a "disciple." This is not only an interesting contrast to the previous healing narrative, where Luke calls Aeneas "a certain man," but it is significant because Tabitha is the only woman in the New Testament specifically accorded that designation. (Luke usually references both men and women disciples together; see Acts 9:1–2, 36; 18:24–26.) These details imply that Tabitha was a well-known and well-respected disciple. I love Tabitha's narrative because she embodied God's heart in taking care of the most vulnerable in her society. Luke says, "Her life overflowed with good works and compassionate acts on behalf of those in need" (Acts 9:36). In a patronage society, her good works gave her the role of benefactor, which would guarantee her special status in the assembly of disciples.[19] She's also mentioned without a husband or sons, which could imply that Tabitha was a widow. This would've put her in the position of marginality— and likely would have made her attuned to God's heart for the marginal in society.

In the narrative, Tabitha becomes ill and dies. Some of the other disciples hear that Peter is nearby in Lydda, so they call for him to come. Perhaps they hope he can, like Jesus, raise people from the dead. When Peter arrives at her bedside, he is met with a room full of widows who are mourning the loss of their dear friend and leader. One of my favorite details in the story lies in the fact that the mourning widows have brought the tunics and other clothing that Tabitha made for them, showing them off to Peter as they mourn (Acts 9:39). Reading this through an abuelita lens highlights the importance of Tabitha's life as a mujer who cared for others through her art making. She was a provider and a healer, a woman who worked with her hands to create and supply.

After Peter sends everyone out of the room, he prays and then tells Tabitha to "get up!" (Acts 9:40).

I wonder, How important was Tabitha's life to the community that not only the widows but the disciples call for Peter to bring her back from the dead? All life has value, of course. I love that we can see this so beautifully in this story: a woman disciple, who is often overlooked in our conversations, was of utmost importance in the story of the early church—so much so, that her life was worthy of resurrection. Besides Tabitha—and Jesus—there are only four other resurrections in the New Testament where a person is named.

After she was raised, Luke tells us that "news spread throughout Joppa" (Acts 9:42). Perhaps her status as one who offered so much financially to the community was subversive, as was the fact that she was a woman providing for herself through her craft. It seems Tabitha dedicated her time on earth to the widows who were now mourning her death. Caring after widows held particular weight in the early church. In fact, just a few chapters prior to Tabitha's story, the Greek-speaking disciples were complaining that the Aramaic-speaking disciples were overlooking their widows in the daily food service (Acts 6). The result was that seven "well-respected" men made sure the widows were looked after. I wonder if word about this important ministry reached Tabitha. Given that her story mentions her Greek name, Dorcas, it's not far off to think she may have caught wind of what was happening among those in her community. Or perhaps Tabitha was well versed in Torah and understood God's heart toward widows.

Additionally, the expression used to describe Tabitha as one who engages in "good works" suggests more than just volunteer work. In Greek, the phrase implies that she exhibits a consistent moral character in her almsgiving, or more specifically, she is a person of compassion. Perhaps this was due to her proximity to pain, to the needs of the community. I wonder if Tabitha not only cared for widows herself but also instructed those in her community on how to properly do so. Dickerson suggests that perhaps she was involved in an early version of union organizing in a sort of volunteer association. This would explain her prominence in the community.[20]

When we speak of Tabitha, it's usually only in relation to Peter and his miracle. We also often mention the widows who were overlooked in Jerusalem; however, we don't typically note the widows who Tabitha took care of in Joppa. Like many abuelita theologians, Tabitha is often overlooked in our conversations about the New Testament and faithful disciples; however, there's enough evidence in the text to tell us that she played a significant role in the early church. And Tabitha isn't alone. In fact, many other early church madrinas used their hands and innovation to not only create entire worlds out of nothing but provide for themselves and others. This often culminated in the gift of hospitality—a virtue that shaped the early church and beyond.

One such example is Lydia, who became the first person in Macedonia to embrace the message of Jesus (Acts 16:15). She was also the first non-Jew to be converted after the Jerusalem Council, which validated the message of Christianity going out to the gentiles (15:28–29).[21] One thing that draws my attention to Lydia is what initially led Paul to her.

While in Troas, before he arrived in Philippi, Paul had a vision of a man begging him to go to Macedonia. "Come over to Macedonia and help us!" (Acts 16:9), the man pleaded in Paul's dream. Luke narrates in Acts 16:10, "Immediately after he saw the vision, we prepared to leave for the province of Macedonia, concluding that God had called us to proclaim the good news to them." Paul, Luke, Timothy, and perhaps others sailed from Troas to Macedonia, stopping at Philippi, "a city of Macedonia's first district and a Roman colony" (v. 12). It was there in Philippi on the Sabbath that Paul—in search of somewhere to pray, perhaps in the hopes that he might be led to the man in his vision—found a group of women (among them Lydia, "a dealer in purple cloth,"

v. 14), who would eventually hear God's message and support Paul's ministry.

Isn't that just like God—to use a vision of a man to get Paul to Philippi and then surprise him with a woman? A woman who was doing what she does, gathering with las mujeres of the neighborhood for prayer on a Sunday afternoon.

Perhaps God wants God's people to be open to surprises—to allow la Espíritu Santa to lead the church in looking for God's activity—through unexpected people and unexpected places, through the faithful abuelas who have been gathering to pray behind the scenes for decades. Like many of our abuelitas, Lydia eventually led her household to accept Paul's message and be baptized. She also invited Paul to stay at her home, engaging in the virtues of hospitality, ready and willing to invite others in for a warm meal, and perhaps even a cafecito.

As mentioned above, Lydia was a "maker and trader of purple cloth" (v. 14). As the head of her household and a businesswoman, Lydia financially supported herself and those in her care. Her leadership even led her to get a group of other "God-fearers," madrinas in the faith, to come together for prayer. In essence, Lydia was a community leader, a woman who worked with her hands—who held ancestral knowledge. She provided, showed hospitality to Paul and those traveling with him, and led the first church in Philippi. Lydia propelled the growth of Christianity in the Roman Empire.[22]

The narratives of these mujeres in Scripture are unique and complex, similar to the human experience. Our stories and our respective cultures are rich and diverse. I said that there is not one abuelita theology but several abuelita theologies, as each of us hold our cultural memories, with all their nuances, in sacred spaces. Just like the Bible is a book of collective voices bearing witness to the liberating love of God, so our collective voices paint the portrait of our ancestors—from the triply marginalized unnamed Canaanite madres to the independent businesswomen who lead churches and run their own companies. Our madrinas guide our imaginations as we engage on our journey of spiritual wholeness, shaped by the embodied knowledge of those who came before us.

I was always fascinated by Abuela's ability to create entire worlds with her hands, and in doing so, she empowered me and dozens of other mujeres in her community. My childhood memories consist of the front door constantly swinging open as Abuela used her skill to serve others and to provide for us. I don't take the knowledge of her hands lightly.

In that, I echo Esther Díaz Martín: "I honor the technologies passed down by my mother and my grandmothers and I find in their knowledge guidance that is not grounded in violence and competition but in creative love and humility."[23] I think this is part of what makes their work an act of resistance against the throes of colonization: it is rooted in deep, radical love.

It is held together by our sacred memories.

Women like Lydia, Tabitha, and las arpilleristas offer us, through the work of their hands, embodied knowledge rooted in compassion for others—those in their communities and those in need of justice. And most importantly, through the work of their hands, our abuelas become the tellers of their own stories.

7

Sobreviviendo

Abuela's dementia took a turn for the worse immediately after the death of her second husband, Mario. Tragedy can have that effect on you. It consumes a person's psyche the way fog devours the epic scenery of the Pacific Coast Highway at daybreak. The beauty, the memories—you know it's all there. It's just not visible because it's masked by the thick, gray mist. In the early stages of dementia, emotional trauma not only clouds the mind; it also hurls the disease forward so quickly that loved ones are left reeling.

The night that Mario died, I had been at church for hours, huddled in a room with three other people planning, strategizing, and swaddling Bibles in hand-me-down clothing like newborn infants. I was prepping for my first trip to the motherland, Cuba, and I was to go as a missionary. Smuggling Bibles in my suitcase and practicing how I'd lie to officials made me feel like a "real" missionary—you know, the kind who is willing to put herself in danger, to be willing to lie to the government for the sake of the "lost."

I hadn't told Abuela that I was going to Cuba. We all knew how she felt about that. Nadie debe visitar a Cuba. Eso solo soporta el gobierno. (No one should visit Cuba. All that does is support the government.)

I was going, however, not to visit world-renowned beaches but to help train pastors and scope out the scene for future missionary endeavors. Even still, I couldn't find it in me to let Abuela know. I convinced myself she wouldn't understand. I was doing this for Jesus. *It's different,* I told myself. *I'm taking the gospel to my own people.* But before our meeting was over, I received a call from Mom telling me the news: Mario was dead.

I immediately rushed home and arrived to a house full of close family, silent, still in shock. What had started off as a seemingly insignificant ear infection killed him in a matter of months.

"You should still go to Cuba," my mom assured me. "We'll be OK." My family had been working so hard to be supportive in my recent transition to evangelicalism, which began when I attended the ONE Conference in Miami.

Several months before attending this conference, I came across a brand-new Christian radio station. Intrigued, I began listening, eventually inviting the sermons and worship songs along with me on my morning commute. After months of engaging with teachings, I became curious to attend the conference that was being promoted. I was in my early twenties, had just graduated from college, and was starting my career as a full-time therapist assistant, making near minimum wage. At that particular moment, I had gone through a bad breakup that left me feeling unsure of my future. Weekdays were marked by full-time work and weekly service projects with a local Catholic church to engage with people experiencing homelessness. On the weekends, I barhopped around Miami with friends and occasionally attended mass on Sundays. Life was good, but like any angsty young adult, I desired adventure and a deeper sense of purpose and belonging—no doubt spurred on by books and memoirs I read in my spare time that detailed spiritual journeys and travel. Perhaps this is what captivated me on that warm and humid February weekend. I showed up to the ONE Conference alone, unsure of what an evangelical worship service or conference looked like after having attended Catholic mass for the majority of my upbringing.

As I waited in the long line at the BankUnited Center on the campus of the University of Miami, I was taken aback by the excitement in so many young people. That initial surprise turned to shock when I sat at my seat and thousands of them began cheering as lasers and lights illuminated the convention center with the word *Jesus* flashing on a jumbotron. I didn't know who Hillsong was at the time, but when they took the stage, hundreds of people flooded to the front of the room, hands up, eyes closed, tears streaming down many of their faces. I remember looking around and thinking, *Where am I? What is this?*

The scene was intriguing enough to lure me back for the second and third days of the conference. Preachers like Francis Chan and Christine Caine shared about making the most of life through mission efforts or organizations like A21, the nonprofit that aims to fight human trafficking.

I didn't need much more convincing after hearing the stories on stage of people giving everything up to find fulfillment and purpose in their service to God and others. The last day of the conference, I serendipitously ran into long-lost family members I hadn't spoken to in years, and they invited me to check out the megachurch they attended. That same week, I visited both their Sunday service and their young adult gathering—and never looked back. I was captivated by the community and belonging and the fact that the majority of young adults dreamed of doing seemingly important things for God. A few months later I attended my first short-term mission trip to El Salvador and began leading my first small group. Not too long after that I quit my job in therapy and began working as a teacher, freeing up my summers to serve as a project leader for a missions organization and lead short-term mission teams across the globe. During the school year I worked full-time throughout the week and led multiple discipleship groups with teens and young adults after school. On the weekends, I ran a youth ministry that I started at an under-resourced church in my area. Life was abundantly full—and seemingly full of purpose. I was all in, albeit exhausted.

Prior to this, I had considered myself a Christian—I believed all of the same things about Jesus—but the passion, emotion, and excitement of this community and the opportunities there were to give of myself felt enthralling. As a learner, I also wanted to immerse myself in all of this new knowledge. I quickly realized there was much to learn about the Bible, and within months I began indulging in books and commentaries to understand its mysteries, stories, and lessons. The opportunity to travel while "serving others" (and being able to raise money to do so!) also appealed to me. Within the first few months as a new evangelical, I had raised enough money to travel to several different countries. I suddenly had a newfound purpose and devotion to God in my life. However, with these feelings came the idea that everything I knew or believed beforehand was wrong. All of my memories with Abuela at St. Dominic's Church, the spiritual retreats I attended in high school, and my communion, confirmation, and relationship to and understanding of the divine before this moment were all lies. None of it was legitimate—I had been deceived by the devil, apparently.

As time passed, I became more and more isolated from my family and friends. Not only was all my time spent at church or church events; I engaged with family and friends only to evangelize them. When they tried to explain to me that they believed in Jesus, I told them that they were mistaken, deceived as I once was. Their Catholic expressions of faith didn't count.

I began to see the people I loved only as objects to convert, and our conversations centered primarily on their sins and their need to repent.

In many ways Mom didn't understand my transition, but she respected it. Before the conference I had leased my first car upon starting my first full-time job, a used Kia Optima. I quickly began to feel guilty about this decision. The books I was reading urged me to be "radical," to live "counterculturally." None of these were particularly bad things; the ideas just didn't go very deep. Much of it played out on the surface.

Many of the messages I received centered on the need to "suffer" for Christ in order to prove genuine devotion. Thus, I thought the only thing I had to my name was too nice, too self-serving. I begged my mom to take over my lease so I could purchase an old Toyota that had a myriad of issues. Mom was able to take over my lease, and I paid for the Toyota in cash with the couple thousand dollars I had saved up from working. Every couple of months I had to scrape together change to fix a part that had broken or needed attention.

Mom didn't understand all of my recent life decisions, but she knew how important it all was to me, which is why she encouraged me to go to Cuba the night that Mario died, instead of staying with the family. She reassured me they, we, would be OK. I knew we, as a family, would, but would I? That night I sat in Abuela's bathroom with my head in my hands and prayed, desperately, *What should I do, God?*

I don't remember what convinced me to stay. All I know is that I couldn't—didn't—get on that plane. I needed to be there para mi familia, for my family.

As dawn approached the next morning, I felt a strange sense of relief. This seemed odd, considering the guilt I was putting myself through, remembering Luke 14:26 about needing to hate my family and myself—which in this case meant leaving them behind even after a recent death—in order to be Jesus's disciple.

However, nothing felt more on par with the life of Jesus the next morning than waking up next to Abuela instead of boarding that plane. Most of the time, "being a disciple" requires we focus on the *being* part, not the doing. But for years, I couldn't put my finger on why I felt relieved not to go to Cuba. I wouldn't understand until years later.

Besides being present with my family, I realized the sobering truth that Cuba didn't need me to save it. It didn't need a wealthy suburban megachurch from Miami to do so either. Years later I learned that the evangelical church in Cuba has been growing exponentially for decades—one of the fastest and largest in the world. The reason? Besides the Holy Spirit, one reason may be that Cubans on the island don't need to peel back layers of privilege to see liberation in the Christian narrative. ¡Libertad! (Freedom!) is a mantra that pumps through the veins of mi gente.

I now know I needed to understand this history and context before stepping foot in the land of my ancestors. I needed to learn to honor and respect them as complex persons with dignity, not one-dimensional subjects to convert. I needed to do a little more reading and a lot more praying about los humildes and about my place as one who is born of them but is very far from their lived experiences.

The night Mario died—the night that interrupted my plans to visit Cuba—would be significant for many reasons. It would be the beginning of the end of the faith journey I thought I had fallen in love with. Abuela's health would begin to decline rapidly, and I would be forced to make sense of it all: life, death, and Jesus. That thick gray mist would soon begin to cloud what I thought I knew about God. I would soon feel that fog of loss that Abuela was familiar with, that she had spent a lifetime straining to see through.

Mario's death wasn't the first time loss had overwhelmed her. Abuela was—is—no stranger to goodbyes; they have always lingered like unwanted guests at the Saturday night domino table.

After saying goodbye to the white sands and clear blue waters of her home country, she bid an unexpected farewell to Papi. Not many years later, Abuela said another goodbye, to her mother, my bisabuela.

The most painful thing about goodbyes is that we're almost never ready for them, and frankly, I don't think they care very much either. Oftentimes they slam the door shut so hard on their way out that they leave you picking up memories off the floor like the shattered bits of a picture frame that fell off the wall from the impact.

One story shaped by widowhood and loss that always captivates me is that of Ruth and Naomi. I know that when it comes to biblical tradition these women aren't unnamed or overlooked in the general sense. However, it's important to highlight their narrative as it's one of the very few in the Hebrew Bible in which women function as protagonistas of their own stories. This is interesting, considering that in the retelling of their stories not only is Boaz somehow front and center, with the point often being that women ought to "wait for their Boaz" (whatever that means), but I've often noticed that many of the details that point to Ruth's and Naomi's wisdom and their agency are often left untold.

I recently received a message from a colleague who is still a student at the first seminary I attended. He told me that in a chapel sermon, the speaker claimed from the pulpit that Naomi "wanted what every woman had ever wanted: a family." I won't go into detail about all the ways this general claim about "every woman" is problematic. But I don't particularly mind the speaker saying Naomi wanted a family—if, and only if, he had also pointed out the reality that older, widowed women during this time literally *needed* family (more particularly men, sons and/or husbands, both of which Naomi lost) in order to *sobrevivir*, to *survive*. This is why Naomi encouraged Ruth to *seduce* Boaz so as to receive a chance at marriage: it was about security. Naomi wanted a family because she didn't want to die, and she was willing to use sex and manipulation for that end. This subtle difference is important, as it highlights Ruth's and Naomi's agency. As Karen González points out in her book *The God Who Sees,* "Ruth and Naomi are poor and vulnerable. But they are not helpless."[1]

Like most other stories in the Bible, this story is complicated and contains many points of contention. Yet this is the reality for many marginalized women: they live in multiple worlds and hold multiple identities and truths. I felt this deeply that night I was preparing for my first trip to Cuba. I was born of them, but my reality is so different from theirs. Would I feel at home when I landed, or even more disconnected from mi gente? Would I seem more American, more Western Christian, than I feel on any given day, when I'm ninety miles across the ocean? Would I reek of privilege and the anti-Black sentiment that was hung heavy on my back like a wet blanket, placed there by many of the white Cubans in Miami who surrounded me—who now look so different from the majority of Afro-Cubans in the motherland and feel themselves superior because of it?

Ruth and Naomi's story begins in Bethlehem, which in Hebrew means "house of bread." Naomi and her husband, Elimelech, and their sons, Mahlon and Chilion, are forced to flee Bethlehem, or the House of Bread, because of—out of all things—a famine. As a result, the family crosses borders and relocates to Moab, where the two sons meet and marry two Moabite women: Ruth and Orpah. This move to Moab would've been controversial, as Moab was the home of the historical enemies of the Israelites— particularly during this time, the period of the judges, when, Scripture says, "all the people did what was right in their own eyes" (Judg. 21:25 ESV). The Moabites, specifically, were thought of as lacking in virtue. For example, when the Israelites left Egypt to head to the promised land and roamed the desert for forty years, it was the Moabites who refused them water. And when the Israelites camped at Beth Peor, some Moabite women tried to seduce the Israelite men into illicit relations and idol worship.[2] This is why Deuteronomy 23:3 is uncompromising about Israelites intermarrying with Moabites. It says, "Moabites can't belong to the LORD's assembly. Not even the tenth generation of such people can belong to the LORD's assembly, as a rule." Some say Elimelech and his family were abandoning their community in a time of need by moving to Moab. Not only were they going to live in the one place that they probably shouldn't have gone, but they did the one thing that they shouldn't have done: intermarry with Moabite women.

Now, a decolonized lens would ask us to think critically about this—namely, the characterization of Moab, particularly of the Moabite women, Ruth and Orpah. To this end, womanist scholar Yolanda Norton points out that Moab in the Hebrew Scriptures is constructed as enduringly carnal, sexual, deviant. For her, this reflects the way that Black female bodies are viewed to this day.[3] This is true for many Indigenous women and other women of color as well. Our bodies have been used and abused by the dominating culture and are often seen as a means of transaction, not different from the way Ruth's own body ends up being used in the story. This is important to note; while this novela—like many other stories in Scripture—can be read as a liberative narrative with regard to women, it also highlights and perpetuates their oppression.

On the one hand, the power, agency, and authority that Ruth takes despite the powers at play are important. On the other hand, an honest look at the text critiques the ways that Ruth engages in her own subjugation for the purpose of survival, as many marginalized women are forced to do. This story is complicated and messy, a true testament to the interstitial space many of us, and our abuelas, inhabit.

Another tension in the story is introduced when Elimelech and his sons suddenly and unexpectedly die. This leaves Naomi in a desperate position, as there was no way for an older woman to support herself without a husband or sons. Her daughters-in-law, Orpah and Ruth, have also lost their husbands, Mahlon and Chilion, which meant they have lost their financial support too. But they are young and could remarry, so they have better chances of survival. Because of this, Naomi suggests what would make the most sense to her daughters-in-law: they should stay with their Moabite families, and Naomi will return to Bethlehem where she came from. However, Naomi's daughters-in-law want to go with her. Ruth tells Naomi that she plans to stick with her. Where Naomi goes, Ruth will go; where Naomi stays, Ruth will stay. While Ruth's declaration is often romanticized in many sermons, I recognize that in a basic sense, it's a simple commitment rooted in survival.

I'd like to make a note about Orpah, an overlooked and dismissed character in the narrative who is often portrayed as selfish—or perhaps as less devoted than Ruth—for listening to her mother-in-law's advice to go back to Moab. A decolonized reading—or perhaps even an abuelita reading—would recognize her story too. For many Indigenous people whose histories are plagued by genocide, Orpah represents women who resist assimilation and colonization by returning home to their people. Additionally, scholars have pointed out that Naomi tells Orpah to return to her *bet 'immah* (her mother's house)—a rare detail in Scripture, as it indicates a family setting identified with the mother rather than the father. When this phrase is used in Scripture, it offers a female perspective on issues that elsewhere are viewed through a male lens.[4]

To this end, Cherokee scholar Laura Donaldson argues that for Cherokee women, Orpah connotes hope because she doesn't reject her traditions or her sacred ancestors. And she chooses the house not only of her clan but of her mother.[5] Donaldson points out the antipatriarchal nature of Cherokee households, which echo the Genesis narrative before the fall. In Genesis 2, after God creates woman and the man calls her such, the text says, "That is why a man leaves his father and mother and is united to his wife, and they become one flesh" (Gen. 2:24 NIV). What's interesting about this passage is that it stands in opposition to traditional patriarchal norms in the ancient world—namely, that women leave their families to join their husbands'. It isn't until after the fall that the patriarchal ordering of the household is introduced. Similarly, in Cherokee households husbands customarily go to live with their wives. And the woman's family, rather than the husband's, becomes the primary caretakers of any children.[6] Reading the Bible through a decolonized lens shines a light on Orpah as more than just a character in passing.

———

Despite Ruth's position as a foreign woman, the text tells us that she shows familial regard for Naomi that wasn't uncommon. In biblical Israel, individual family members were typically embedded in the domestic group both economically and psychologically. In premodern societies, the concept of the individual as we know it today did not yet exist.[7] Perhaps this is what led Ruth to feel the way she did for Naomi. Or perhaps she saw a woman deeply grieving, an older widow who would be left destitute, without a chance to remarry. I wonder if this led her to experience a deep-rooted sense of compassion.

I often think of how the Hebrew word for *compassion* comes from the same root word as *womb*. This reminds me that compassion is an embodied experience formed in one of the most intimate parts of the human body, and it must be birthed and nurtured from inside of us into the world. In his book *Just Mercy*, Bryan Stevenson talks about how proximity brings forth—births— compassion. Love requires that we be up close and personal to pain.[8] Perhaps Ruth feels compassion for Naomi because she is proximate to her pain, allowing it to form and take shape inside of her. Our fight for justice requires we do the same.

I can't imagine that Ruth's decision to stay with Naomi is an easy one. She is a Moabite thinking of moving to Bethlehem, somewhere she wouldn't particularly be welcomed. For Israel and the biblical world, ethnicity was a matter of social organization around particular norms.[9] Perhaps this is why, when Ruth establishes her commitment to Naomi, Naomi doesn't respond. The text says that "she stopped speaking to her about it" (Ruth 1:18). Is she worried about what might happen if she brings a foreign woman back to her people?[10]

After they arrive in Bethlehem, however, Ruth and Naomi begin coming up with plans to ensure their survival. The first involves Ruth gleaning by the fields "behind someone in whose eyes [she] might find favor" (Ruth 2:2). She eventually meets Boaz, which prompts Naomi to devise a second plan, more cunning and clever than the first. Naomi encourages Ruth to dress up, put on perfume, wait till Boaz is drunk, then sneak into his bedroom, and seduce him.

Ruth's plan eventually works, and their futures are secured. However, we might pause to think about *how* this is achieved, how two women enact their agency within a patriarchal world. If this story is so common, then why isn't Ruth and Naomi's cleverness highlighted, celebrated, told, and retold time and again? Why are their actions mostly silenced, and why are Boaz's most often focused on?

Like so many stories of the women in the Bible, not only does God bless Ruth and Naomi's seemingly questionable acts, but this story is recorded in Scripture, as are many other cunning and clever acts among the powerless. As Indian American scholar Michelle Reyes says, "For the powerless in the world—in places where there is no such thing as equality and rights for all, when things like educational access and benefactors and social mobility are impossible, when the powerful are cruel—what do the powerless have at their disposal to protect them? Oftentimes nothing but the power of their own voice and their choice of agency."[11]

Becoming a "trickster," as it is typically called in folklore and mythology, is not an anomaly in Scripture. In fact, many women in the Bible and in our society who experience marginalization are forced to find a new "wisdom" to ensure their survival.[12] Like Ruth, a trickster has "low or relatively lower social status, prohibiting gain or advancement through means available to others." This means that "a trickster has to employ wit and cunning to achieve the desired end."[13] Feminist biblical scholar Phyllis Trible argues that Naomi is a bridge between tradition and innovation, and both Ruth and Naomi act as human agents who manifest divine providence by their own acts, very much like Shiprah, Puah, and Jochebed in Exodus.[14]

In many cases, desperate people must engage in what Miguel De La Torre calls an "ethical praxis of jodiendo."[15] Admittedly, in Spanish the word *joder* is a vulgar word used in informal conversation—a word most of our abuelitas probably wouldn't want us to utter. Essentially, it means "screw it" or to "screw with" the system. What De La Torre describes is an ethics that screws with the prevailing power structures to create instability within structures of oppression.

Reading Scripture critically allows us to see the divine joderon in our beloved characters, many of whom are women, and all of whom are blessed by God because of their ability to sobrevivir. As De La Torre puts it, "Joderones become tricksters who lie to reveal truth. They lie, cheat, joke, and deceive to unmask deeper truths obscured by the dominant culture's moralists. Such liberative praxis may be dismissed as immoral by the dominant culture; still, tricksters remain ethical, operating in a realm beyond good and evil, beyond what society defines as right or wrong. Joderones are consummate survivors, serving as exemplars for the disenfranchised in need of surviving the reality of disenfranchisement."[16]

I want to add to De La Torre's ethics the role of *women*, which involves their sexuality. Many women in Scripture must use their sexuality because it is through their sexuality that they are marginalized and subjected to abuse. They use their sexuality as a means to maintain an ambiguous relationship to patriarchy, as they both preserve and undermine established power structures.[17]

There are few women who embody this more clearly than Tamar in Genesis 38. Tamar is a Canaanite woman and the daughter-in-law of Judah. She is chosen by her father-in-law to marry his eldest son, Er, but Scripture says Er was "wicked in the Lord's sight; so the Lord took his life" (Gen. 38:7 NIV). In this culture, it was customary for a woman to marry the brother of her deceased husband in order to be provided for and remain a part of the family. This Levirate law was put in place to protect a childless widow from destitution by guaranteeing that a man who died without children would still acquire offspring perceived by the community to be the dead man's heir.[18] So Tamar is then married to Judah's second son, Onan. However, when Onan lies with Tamar, he spills his semen on the ground, refusing to comply with the Levirate custom of producing his dead brother's offspring. This act leads to Onan's death, making Tamar twice widowed.

Now Tamar is supposed to marry Judah's third son, Shelah. But seeing what happened to his first two sons, Judah lies to Tamar, sends her back home, and tells her to wait there until Shelah is old enough to marry her—but he has no intention of actually carrying out the marriage. Instead, he leaves Tamar abandoned without a husband or offspring. Her situation is particularly dire because she is not legally free to marry anyone else as long as a brother of her husband is alive. Thus Tamar is left as a banished, childless widow without property. She lacks security and perhaps feels hopeless, fearful, or even angry. Tamar has been deprived of her rights and means of survival by those in power. All she has left are her body, her agency, and her ingenuity, and she essentially puts to use her remaining resources.[19]

Years pass, and Tamar realizes Shelah is grown up and hasn't been given to her in marriage. Knowing she's been played, left as a widow without husbands or sons to protect her, she takes off her widow's clothes, covers herself with a veil, and sits down on the road to Timah, a place Judah passes on the way to shear his sheep. Judah sees her, thinks she's a prostitute, and asks to sleep with her. Tamar asks him what his payment will be for sex, and he tells her that he will give her a young goat from his flock. Tamar requests a pledge until she gets her goat, so he gives her his seal, cord, and staff he's holding. After they have sex and Judah sends someone to bring her a goat in order to get his pledge back, Tamar is nowhere to be found. Months later, Tamar finds out she is pregnant, and once her pregnancy is discovered, she is brought to Judah. He attempts to exercise his prerogative to burn her to death, but she shows him the seal, cord, and staff, saying she is pregnant by the man who owns them. Judah recognizes his items and declares, "She's more righteous than I am, because I didn't allow her to marry my son Shelah" (Gen. 38:26).

In this story, Tamar's trickery awards her the title of "righteous." She secures a future for herself. And the best part? Her son, Perez, is the ancestor of King David and Jesus, gaining her a place in Jesus's genealogy as described in the first chapter of Matthew. Tamar also exemplifies a sabiduría, a wisdom, that includes keeping track of Judah. Not only did she know where he'd be, but it seems she might have had a spy or an insider to keep her in the loop. Thus, Tamar's knowledge about Judah and the strategy of playing the harlot turned her from the passive victim to the active arbiter of her own fate.[20] What an image: *Jesus Christ born from the trickery and deceit of an abuelita theologian jodiendo the system in order to secure her survival.*

Mario died only six years after he and Abuela married. I remember their wedding day as if it were yesterday. Our immediate familia huddled in the living room of Abuela's duplex on the outskirts of Little Havana. We were giddy and teary eyed as we waited for her to emerge out of her bedroom and walk down the dozen or so steps through the living room toward her groom. He wore his crisp white guayabera (a traditional Cuban dress shirt), and she wore a pink and white pantsuit.

Mario was visibly nervous, shaking, and I will never forget the look he wore on his wrinkly, worn face. Have you ever seen pure contentment? It looks like a ninety-three-year-old man finally marrying the woman he's spent thirty years head over heels in love with. This was the moment he had waited nearly a lifetime for, and we all knew what it meant, particularly to him.

While this scene was as endearing as you can imagine, imprinted on my memory forever, the grander narrative is— unsurprisingly—more complicated. Mario had proposed to Abuela nearly a dozen times since that first night they met at their church's choir practice in the late 1970s. He knew he wanted to marry her for decades, but her response was always a firm no. Abuela was clear that she didn't need a man to provide or protect her. She had been surviving la lucha all on her own. To this day, I admire her willingness to stick to her truth: "Roberto [Papi] siempre será mi único amor" (Roberto will always be my only love).

For over twenty years Abuela held on to this truth, not wavering until the very end, when it became a matter of survival.

Abuela and Mario met only a few years after they both arrived in this country and coincidently lost their spouses around the same time. I imagine they found comfort within the stained-glass windows of St. Dominic's Church. The sacrament of holy Eucharist, the recitations of Hail Marys and the petitioning for intercession of San Lazaro (St. Lazarus)—the patron saint of lepers and Cuba's favorite saint—all were intimate reminders of a home and a life once lived. Their friendship was birthed from goodbyes—both to their spouses and their home country—and sustained by each other's company. Throughout the years, hope found its home within the cracked pieces of two broken hearts that came together to form the semblance of a whole one.

I imagine that Mario fell in love with Abuela because of her resilience. Who wouldn't? Oftentimes, strength is borrowed. When we can't muster any of our own strength, riding the wave of someone else's becomes our saving grace. Perhaps this is who Abuela was for Mario. I realize now this is who she was for me— my matriarchal powerhouse. While this reality is beautiful, it also stings. The abuelitas in our lives—those whose faith and strength shaped us—often carry unbelievably heavy burdens, and most of the time they're expected to, without hesitation.

For nearly thirty years, Mario never gave up on winning Abuela over. Sure, he was in the perpetual "friend zone," akin to the hopeless-romantic teenage boys on TV. But for some reason, being the best friend is sometimes better than being nothing at all.

Things remained this way until one unexpected night in 2008. Mario was sent to the hospital with—of all things—a chronic case of the hiccups. He was in his early nineties and, up until this point, had been going strong—driving, jogging, coming over to Abuela's house to play dominoes on most nights, and taking her salsa dancing on the others. He routinely visited each day after work, and Abuela would cook him one enormous meal—this meal being the only thing he would eat every afternoon. Perhaps one of these massive daily feedings is how he initially came down with the hiccups.

Mario didn't have a close relationship with his family; during the twenty years I knew him, I never once met any of his family members. I don't know exactly why. Growing up, I assumed it was because of his devotion to Abuela. Either way, Mario's commitment to Abuela earned him an intimate place in our familia. He became the abuelo I didn't get the opportunity to meet. Sometimes he taught me how to do things—like sharpen my lead pencils with a pocket knife—like they did en el campo (the countryside).

Years later I would teach him how to do things, like add contacts to his new flip phone.

The night that Mario was sent to the hospital was the night Abuela decided she would marry him. I saw the despair on Abuela's face as she sat by him in the bed, tubes down his throat. I had never seen such a resilient person look so pitiful. The creases on her face were deep with worry.

I thought that seeing her closest friend and deepest admirer on a hospital bed with cords hanging out of his arms and mouth had sparked something in her that had been dormant for too long. I thought the realization that his time on earth was short led her to recognize her love for him. Perhaps this was part of it, but I learned with time that her anxiety was also due to Mario's lack of support. She was it. Where were his children, grandchildren? Why didn't they care? How could they let their elderly father wither away by himself?

Who would make legal decisions for him after he could no longer make them for himself?

When she told me she finally decided to marry him, I was over the moon. "My elderly grandparents are *getting married!*" I told everyone willing to share in the joy over my news. As a young, hopelessly romantic college student, I thought for the first time that true love could actually exist.

But years later I found out the real reason why Abuela decided to marry Mario. While I wanted to be disappointed at the fact that it wasn't about realized romantic feelings or missed opportunities, I just couldn't. Why? Because upon hearing her reasoning, I realized a few things. First, I realized the kind of woman Abuela is, how she embodied genuine love. Second, I realized that life and the outworking of love are more complicated than what I had envisioned while being raised on Disney movies. Oftentimes, it has everything to do with sobreviviendo.

The reality is that Abuela married Mario because she wanted to be legally able to sign for him the next time he wound up in the hospital. For a majority of her life, Abuela resisted the traditional notion of marriage, only to turn it on its head in the end.

In that hospital room she had, in fact, been reminded that life is short and fragile—and it was her turn to love Mario the way he had loved her for so long. So the day after Mario left the hospital, he heard the words he had waited nearly a lifetime to hear: "Vamos a casarnos" (Let's get married). Knowing Mario was going to die sooner than later, Abuela was willing to become doubly widowed, a position that comes with its own marginalization. Why would she choose to do that?

For Abuela—and many women like her—love makes decisions based on desperate circumstances. It steps in when others won't, and it sticks around. It provides comfort and a sense of belonging when it's needed most. Abuela married Mario before his death, but not because she needed a man to provide for her or because she wanted to enjoy pleasure or companionship. Abuela shamed the traditional notions of marriage, as well as what was expected of her—namely, committing and submitting to a man who would protect and provide for her.

More specifically, Abuela shamed the entire system by marrying for legal purposes. Like many other people attempting to survive throughout history, Abuela wielded marriage as a tool so she could step in and do the right thing, to fight for Mario when no one else would. Throughout the years, Mario had become familia, and familia sacrifices for you. Familia will go through unimaginable measures to shame powers or systems that get in the way. And the most overwhelming aspect of this is that God responds to the measures marginalized women take when it comes to sacrifice and survival. Abuela used marriage not in its traditional way, not to play the role of traditional wife and mother, but to be the one to provide.

She played the game of the system in order to bring justice.

The story of Esther is wildly subversive, engaging trickery and wisdom, both in Esther's actions and in the narrative as a whole. Besides the book of Ruth, the book of Esther is the only other book-length narrative in the Hebrew Bible that revolves around a female character.[21] Like Ruth, Esther seeks to ensure survival and continuity, but in her case, this is enacted on a grand scale, redeeming not just her family but a whole branch of the Jewish nation. In her story, Esther is celebrated for saving the Jews of Persia from genocide.[22] But at the same time, as many feminist commentators point out, she participates in patriarchy by doing things like stressing the king's authority and waiting patiently and obediently until his permission is granted in order to speak. I understand the need to wrestle with this as we reflect on and engage with her story—namely, that Esther liberates a nation but has to bow to the oppressive powers, to patriarchy, to do so.

Throughout history, this has been a reality for many women, particularly women of color. In the past, their need to survive in a world not meant for them has forced them to be subversive, to play the empire's game. I believe this has been a part of the sabiduría of our abuelitas and our colonized ancestors: sometimes they bow to authority in order to disrupt it. Some of the grandest narratives in Scripture exist in these complicated and interstitial spaces. Of course this isn't true across the board. As Lady Wisdom reminds us in Proverbs, sometimes you don't answer a fool according to their folly or you'll be just like them (26:4), and sometimes you do or else you'll make them think they're wiser than they are (26:5).

Scripture and the abuelita theologians found within it remind us that wisdom is contextual, situational. And lo cotidiano, the everyday lived experiences of marginalized people, is complex and nuanced, without the clear black and white that fundamentalist religion wants us to believe exists.

Despite the complicated spaces abuelas throughout history have inhabited, these narratives teach us an overwhelming truth about God: that God is on the side of the oppressed and that God is for the liberation of those on the margins.

Neither Esther, Ruth, nor Tamar are military or political leaders like Deborah or Jael. Neither are they prophets or thinkers in the way we traditionally understand these terms. What distinguishes Ruth and Esther, particularly from a narrative perspective, is that they seemingly lack awareness of God; their stories omit reference to the divine. In the book of Esther, even though God isn't mentioned, it's obvious that God's presence pumps through the veins of the story.

The more I've heard the stories of abuelita theologians in our midst, the more I recognize that God doesn't need to be explicitly named to be at work. In fact, God can be found in the complicated aspects of these stories. In our theological imaginations, we understand God to be there, present, even—and perhaps especially—in their deceit. Many Christians are uncomfortable admitting this, because we've built an image of what we think God is like. But when we look at the actions of desperate people, particularly women, it shatters our preconceived notions of the divine. In this way, God is in the details.

As divine joderones, women like Ruth, Tamar, and Esther work in society to uncover its inconsistencies, inequalities, and injustices. The paradox is found in that while they deceive, they also tell the truth. They do this by exposing the deficiencies of what *is* and offering an opportunity to see what *could be*—seeking justice not just for themselves but oftentimes for a group or society as a whole. Even in adversity and oppression, women are capable of jodiendo their way into more desirable positions. But most important, these trick*stars* (as they've been called) can make life better for men as well as for women by using tricks to gain advantages for their communities—and being blessed by God because of it.[23]

8

Protesta and Persistence

On May 25, 2020, footage was released detailing the murder of George Floyd by Minneapolis police. The video was released after the back-to-back murders of other Black Americans, including Ahmaud Arbery and Breonna Taylor. The video's release happened smack-dab in the middle of the global COVID-19 pandemic, when millions of businesses were closed and people across the world were forced to stay home in an effort to stop the spread of the virus.

The ongoing murder of innocent Black people along with mandated stay-at-home orders provided the perfect recipe for upheaval. For centuries, Black people across America have been saying enough is enough. This wasn't the first time they, alongside allies, took to the streets, but thanks in part to social media and the many videos documenting the murder of Black people that have surfaced in recent years, something felt different. Protests erupted across the country for weeks on end, reaching unprecedented places, including Harrison, Arkansas, one of the most historically racist cities in the country. A hub for the Ku Klux Klan, Harrison held its first Black Lives Matter protest, where mostly white people from across the small city joined together to stand against systemic racism.

As I reflected on the news cycle, attended protests, and wrestled with how an abuelita faith could speak to this moment, I couldn't help thinking of the Black mothers and grandmothers who have had to disproportionately bury their sons and daughters—those who have been protesting since before I existed and still others who are organizing and protesting today. For example, one such group is the Mothers of the Movement, which is made up of the mothers of Black men and women—including Trayvon Martin, Michael Brown, Eric Garner, and Sandra Bland—who have died at the hands of police, in police custody, or from gun violence.[1] The Mothers of the Movement began as a result of the 2013 acquittal of George Zimmerman after he shot and killed Trayvon Martin.[2]

Reflecting on these mothers, I immediately remembered one mother's protest that also changed the course of history: Rizpah.

Rizpah came to mind after I saw a poster by Rachel Costa that went viral. It reads, "All mothers were summoned when George Floyd called out for his mama"[3]—referencing the video of Floyd's final breaths in which he is heard calling out to his mother. The sign—sparked by Floyd's last words—drew a visceral response from moms all over the world for many different reasons. For me, it also had a deep theological core.

I wouldn't be surprised if you haven't heard about Rizpah. It took me many years of reading the Bible before I discovered her. And when attempting to gain more insight about her, I became disheartened by how little information is available. With a book (the Bible) so old and so widely read—usually multiple times by the same person—you'd think more attention would be paid to a character like Rizpah, one whose story, although short, shaped the history of Israel. The fact that Rizpah's story is generally unknown can be discouraging, but it isn't surprising. It's common for the dominant culture to overlook bodies on the margins.

In order for us to recognize abuelita theologians in Scripture, we must continue to re-center those who have been ignored or pushed aside, because God often resides most powerfully among the most powerless.

Despite being a minor character, Rizpah played a major role. While her story takes up only a few short passages, her presence is undeniable—jumping from the pages of Scripture. I've found this to be true with many overlooked women in the Bible.

Rizpah appears twice in the book of 2 Samuel. In her first appearance in 3:6–11, we learn about the circumstance she finds herself in, a situation in which she is being used as a pawn in the great game of kings.[4] Her body is a site of contention for the monarchy after Saul's death.[5] When we first learn about her, she is a victim caught in a web of male domination, power, and sex. This is not unique to Rizpah or to the women of this time. Many marginalized bodies are still disregarded, abused, and misused today. Sexual violence in the US disproportionately impacts women of color, immigrant women, LGBTQIA+ women, and disabled women. At the US southern border, migrant women and girls are the victims of sexual assaults. They exist in the shadows of the #MeToo movement, as the abuse of migrant women at the border often goes unreported, uninvestigated, and unprosecuted.[6]

The bodies of Black, Indigenous, and other women of color have been eroticized for centuries, their sexuality used as a weapon—many enduring rape as part of European colonization. To this day, Indigenous women in the United States are 2.5 times more likely to be sexually assaulted than other women.[7] After the Philippine-American War, World War II, and the Korean and Vietnam wars, the US occupation in Asian countries propelled local sex trafficking rings to serve soldiers. Black women were routinely sexually assaulted during slavery in the United States, as a "weapon of domination" with the goals of lessening enslaved women's will to resist and of demoralizing their men. The institutionalized rape of Black women endured after slavery, with the Ku Klux Klan and other oppressive groups using rape to reinforce the oppression of the Black community.

Rizpah's story of abuse and misuse is one story among many. She was King Saul's concubine and the mother of two of his sons. A concubine was akin to a mistress and merited a status lower than that of other women. Concubines were included among the spoils of war, often awarded like trophies to victors.[8]

Rizpah's first cameo is short. We don't learn much about her other than the fact that one of Saul's sons, Ishbosheth, is accusing Saul's army general, Abner, of sleeping with her. During this time, sleeping with a king's concubine was akin to attempting to usurp his throne, making Rizpah a casualty of the bloody business of king making.[9]

Womanist scholar Wilda Gafney points out two important details about the accusation: (1) the unprotected woman would have had no choice of consent, and (2) when accused of raping Rizpah, Abner doesn't deny it. Instead, his response to the accusation (2 Sam. 3:8–10) is to rage, list his past support for Saul's house, and promise to help God keep a divine oath to elevate David.[10]

Because the author isn't filling us in on Rizpah's thoughts or feelings concerning this encounter, I wonder, How did she feel? Did anyone defend her? Did God condone such an act from those in power, those who were put in place to lead God's people? Asking these sorts of questions not only tunes our ears to listen more intently but sharpens our gaze and softens our hearts toward the vulnerable. In her book *Inspired*, Rachel Held Evans urges that we train ourselves to ask hard questions about the Bible. If we emotionally distance ourselves from any potential conflicts or doubts, then we won't find the courage to challenge interpretations that justify injustice.[11] Mirroring this sentiment, Eugene Peterson says, "We don't become more spiritual by becoming less human."[12] To be more like Jesus is not to be less emotional and more disengaged from the messiness of the world (or Scripture). It's the opposite.

Asking hard questions about the Bible also mirrors the discipline of our Jewish siblings. To them, being without questions is a sign not of faith but of lack of depth.[13] If Judaism is a religion of questions, then we as Christians should also seek to ask them as we read the Hebrew Scriptures.

Rizpah's story, and the situation thereof, is complicated. She is presented as a woman without agency. But as we keep reading, her story takes an unexpected turn, reappearing in 2 Samuel 21:1–14. When Rizpah is introduced for the second time, not only do we learn a little bit more about her character, but something important happens: she becomes the protagonista of her own story.

By the time we reach chapter 21, years have passed, and it's now late during David's reign as king. The nation of Israel is in a three-year drought and famine. David—curious about the circumstances—decides to inquire of God why the Israelites are suffering without food or water. To David's surprise, God informs him that his predecessor, King Saul, was at fault because he broke a treaty made with the Gibeonites during his reign. This treaty had been important, as it ensured that the Gibeonites would be protected and secure in their land.

Instead of keeping his end of the deal, however, Saul attempted to exterminate the Gibeonites from Israel. What made this situation even more complicated was that in ancient Israel, when innocent blood was shed, it always needed to be avenged.

After learning about this important piece of history, David decides to go to the offended Gibeonites and ask what they would require to vindicate the unjust murder of their people so that God would end the famine. The Gibeonites decide that they want seven sons from the house of Saul. David, choosing to spare his beloved Jonathan's son, hands over Rizpah's two sons, Mephibosheth and Armoni, along with the five sons of Saul's older daughter, Merab. The Gibeonites take the young men and essentially lynch them, leaving the bodies of Saul's sons and grandsons to rot, exposed and humiliated in the presence of God at a local shrine.[14] This is a particularly vile and insulting punishment, as it also violates Israelite burial practices. Not only was decent burial greatly important in ancient Israel, but the law maintained that burial should always take place before sunset.[15]

I want to circle back to Rizpah as my theological imagination begins churning, imagining what an atrocious circumstance this was for her. Not only were her sons murdered; they were left degraded and exposed to rot in the heat of the sun and to be devoured by wild animals.

I can't fathom the agony and desperation Rizpah felt.

On top of losing her children, she lost her financial security, as women relied on the men in their family to provide for them. Rizpah faced complete and utter destitution. Because she was also intimately aligned with the house of Saul—who was considered a rival of David—some argue that she was probably socially ostracized and treated as a political outcast.[16]

But in the midst of this sorrow, Rizpah does something radical and remarkable.

She takes action by asserting herself, choosing to act not only in bravery but also in justice. Scripture tells us that Rizpah took appropriate funeral clothing, spread it out by a rock, and stayed at the scene of the execution "from the beginning of the harvest until the rains poured down on the bodies from the sky"—about six months—in an act of protest. Scripture says, "She wouldn't let any birds of prey land on the bodies during the day or let wild animals come at nighttime" (2 Sam. 21:10).

Rizpah puts her life, her misused and abused marginalized body, on the line to seek justice for her own children's violated bodies. She wanted justice, and she dared to believe that God wanted justice too.

I wonder if anyone helped her, brought her food, or stayed with her to keep her company. I can't imagine the smell of her sons' bodies as they stiffened, bloated, and dissolved into decay, or the look of death the decomposing bodies possessed after months of rotting in the sun. I picture Rizpah exhausted, yelling through a hoarse voice and dried tears, waving her arms frantically to prevent vultures from ripping the flesh from her sons' corpses. I imagine her trembling as hungry predators' peering yellow eyes haunt her. I picture her dry, leathery skin parched, begging for respite under the blazing heat of the desert by day and the freezing cold by night.

Rizpah is considered an activist, one who not only took action to seek justice for the bodies but boldly shamed the king for not properly burying Saul and his sons.

But the story doesn't end there. King David heard about Rizpah's vigil, and moved by her actions, he decided to order that the bodies of the young men, along with the bodies of both King Saul and Jonathan, be given a proper and decent burial.

It was only after this that the famine ended.

Lynching the men did not heal the land or save the people; doing right by a wronged woman did.[17] As Robin Branch says, "Mere vengeance was not enough to appease God. There had to be mercy—and justice—as well."[18]

Oftentimes the most overlooked and untold stories are those that teach us the greatest lessons and offer the truest examples of faith rooted in survival, strength, and resistance. More than that, they're stories in which the seemingly powerless will stand up to power in an attempt to right wrongs.

Rizpah understood and embodied those abuelita values and the abuelita faith that God wants us all to live out: "He has told you, O mortal, what is good; and what does the LORD require of you but to do justice, and to love kindness, and to walk humbly with your God?" (Mic. 6:8 NRSV). Rizpah not only impacted the political powers that be but brought the waters to rain down from heaven, saving thousands of hungry and thirsty lives.

Rizpah is not alone. In many ways, she—alongside Shiprah, Puah, and Jochebed—acts as a foremother of civil disobedience and peaceful protest. Since the time of ancient Israel, mothers and abuelas have been engaging in similar acts.

Las Madres de la Plaza de Mayo was a group of mamás y abuelas that formed in la Plaza de Mayo in Argentina to protest their children being abducted by the antidemocratic military regime that ruled in Argentina from 1976 to 1983. The mothers' tragic stories began in 1976, when the Argentine military toppled the presidency of Isabel Perón. The military junta that took power was part of a larger series of political coups called Operation Condor, a campaign that was sponsored and supported by the US.[19]

The new military dictatorship resulted in the Dirty War, which was ultimately an attack against the Argentinean people. State-sponsored torture and terrorism targeted those the regime called the "subversives," which were mostly young university students involved in activism and social projects that included human rights programs that engaged the poor. The government had labeled these "ideological dissidents" (as many called them) as Marxists. Many of the Madres explained that their children were not guerrillas or terrorists but historians, anthropologists, and sociologists. One young doctor had been tagged a "subversive" for offering medical help to the poor in Tucumán.

During this time, over thirty thousand men, women, and children were kidnapped in their homes or on the street by military police both in uniform and in plain clothes. Those kidnapped were sent to clandestine concentration camps or torture centers, never to be seen again. Many were drugged and dropped from planes into the ocean; others were baked in ovens. Many women were impregnated by rape, and after they gave birth, their children were trafficked, mostly to military families.

The Madres started organizing in 1977 when the rest of the public remained silent and terrorized over the hellish things that were taking place. Representing different races and classes and a range of cultural, religious, and political views, the Madres began meeting at the Plaza de Mayo, where the presidential palace was located. They had tried everything to seek justice for their children, visiting the police station regularly to file reports and demanding that someone tell them what was going on. When nothing seemed to work, they committed to meet every Thursday at la plaza, defying the law that prohibited public meetings. The group began with just fourteen people and continued to grow.

Renée Epelbaum remembers the fear she felt at first, as she tirelessly looked for her missing son. After her second son was kidnapped, she decided that enough was enough—"Ya, basta de miedo" (Enough with fear), she said. "No debo de tener miedo, y salí a la calle" (I shouldn't be afraid, and I left for the street).[20]

Las Madres then began to take the streets. One Madre admits that when they began meeting, they didn't even know what they wanted to do at the plaza. It began as a movement of solidarity among mothers, knowing they were each in the struggle together; they weren't alone. Perhaps in that time they hoped they could speak to the president or someone who would listen and tell them about their children. While many admitted they were afraid, they went to the plaza in an effort to seek justice. "Era nuestra obligación y desesperación" (It was our obligation and our desperation).[21] For las Madres, going to the plaza meant overcoming fear, the fear that had silenced the rest of the population.

Eventually las Madres grew to hundreds and then thousands of mothers who continued to meet and protest every Thursday, marching, chanting, and holding up signs of their lost loved ones. However, they were regularly met by military soldiers with combat gear and rifles who began arresting these mothers. They put inflammatory ads in the paper, graffitied the city with information about them, cut and tapped their phone lines. In late 1977 the large group of mothers met at a church to pray, and there dozens of them were also kidnapped, including a French nun who had been helping their cause, as well as the leader of the group at that time, Azucena de Vincenti. The dictatorship thought that perhaps this would silence the mothers, but it only emboldened them. "They couldn't measure the mother's love," said Epelbaum, "nor our desperation."[22] There was no longer one Azucena but hundreds and then thousands of them.

A second group, las Abuelas de Plaza de Mayo, began organizing alongside the Madres. Las Abuelas began to demand justice for their missing grandchildren, the ones born in the custody of the government. Las Madres and Abuelas began petitioning churches to use their influence to find out about their missing children, but the vast majority of churches remained silent. Another leader of the group, Hebe de Bonafini, explained, "The role of the church hierarchy has been unfortunate, because with its silence it has caused more young people to disappear. We asked them to raise their voices but they didn't do it."[23] Out of eighty-three bishops, only three supported las Madres.

Las Madres began approaching world leaders, and mothers from across the globe began taking notice. Women in Holland, Canada, France, Italy, Spain, and other countries began mobilizing and visiting the mothers in Argentina, adding to their numbers and protesting in front of embassies in their countries every Thursday in solidarity with las Madres. Mothers from across the globe also sent money. Las Madres opened an official center to organize their weekly protests and provide assistance to the grandmothers who were left raising the grandchildren of their disappeared children. Eventually Chile, Guatemala, Honduras, Peru, Lebanon, and other countries joined in.

The Argentinean mothers were able to make the stories of their kidnapped children world news, no longer hidden but exposed. Throughout this time, however, many Western democracies continued to sell arms to Argentina, including the US, which was a leading supplier until President Jimmy Carter's human rights campaign. Over three thousand Argentinean officers were trained at the School of the Americas in Panama, a recognized US army service school that trained Latin American students with US doctrine and tactics.

In 1983 the regime was defeated by a new president who eventually paid attention to las Madres for the first time, their campaign now won over by young people. However, when the young Madres wanted to judge the military for its crimes, the government was slower to act, telling them it would destabilize the new government.

In an interview in 1999, Nora Morales de Cortiñas explained that, prior to getting engaged with the movement, she was a "traditional wife, a homemaker." Her husband was "a patriarchal man" who didn't agree with her newfound passion in the political sphere. "We had to get used to public life, new relationships, the loss of privacy, traveling a lot, using different forms of speech, preparing ourselves to meet with people in power, speaking to the media, and being recognized in the street," says Cortiñas.[24] She explained that the resistance of women and housewives alone, without men, made the dictatorship uncomfortable. The power she found in this group of women motivated and empowered Cortiñas to earn a degree in social psychology, and she eventually served as the head of the Open Department of Economic Power and Human Rights at the School of Economics of the University of Buenos Aires.

These mothers and abuelas, a group of unknown women whom the government attempted to silence due to their consistent demands to see their children alive, generated a different form of political consciousness through collective action. In taking these bold steps, las Madres also transformed the classic values associated with politics and motherhood. The protests led them into public life, opening the way for new forms of civic participation. Las Madres took motherhood, a role once reserved for the home, into the public arena of politics, political mobilization, and confrontation. In this way, las Madres challenged and politicized traditional roles, giving them new values. "Given the responsibility for conserving life, they demanded the rights inherent in their obligations, thereby politicizing their personal relationships and their consciousness as women." They also adopted the slogan "Our children gave birth to us," with many of them explaining that their children's lives changed them, making them aware of human rights violations and the value and importance of social activism.[25]

Las Abuelas de Plaza de Mayo, through their persistence, were able to push the government to establish a national genetic data bank to store the genetic profiles of families seeking missing children. Less than a decade after they started meeting, the Banco Nacional de Datos Genéticos (the National Bank of Genetic Data) was established. As of 2019, they have located 130 missing grandchildren.

A similar group of women began meeting in Cuba in 2003 after the Cuban government arrested, tried, and sentenced seventy-five human rights defenders, independent journalists, and librarians.[26] The wives, mothers, and relatives of the jailed dissidents began meeting every Sunday after attending mass and praying for their relatives in Santa Rita church in Havana. Their group became known as las Damas de Blanco (the Ladies in White) because they were marked by their white outfits, which were chosen to symbolize peace. They marched down the streets of Havana in peaceful protest of the unjust incarceration of their loved ones.

Hundreds of las Damas were arrested, harassed, and threatened for protesting peacefully. For example, Ivonne Malleza Galano and her husband were arrested in 2010 for holding a banner that read, "Stop hunger, misery and poverty in Cuba." In 2012, seventy of las Damas were arrested without charges on their way to or from mass. Later in that same year, 100 to 150 of them were placed under house arrest.

While arrests continued throughout 2015 and 2016, las Damas persisted in their fight for justice. Like las Madres and Abuelas de la Plaza de Mayo, they refused to give up.

At the height of the George Floyd protests many people woke up to systemic injustices for the first time. Others who had been sounding the alarm for decades were finally met with understanding. But as the latter have pointed out, seeking justice is a lifelong commitment that requires continual effort. For those of us who are not Black, this means that we must consistently assess our own lives and communities—especially the biases and prejudices that inform our worldviews.

As Christians, we all must seek to live holistic lives. This means that we must constantly evaluate how we might be participating— both personally and systemically—in practices that plague others. I know I am always having to look internally at my ways of being and understanding the world that might perpetuate injustice— from evaluating my prejudices to my spending habits, and from whom I learn from to how I care for creation. It's an ongoing effort that I must commit to until I meet my ancestors in el cielo, in heaven.

To this day, las Madres and Abuelas are still demanding justice. Nearly fifty years later, they still meet every Thursday at la plaza; many of them are in their eighties and nineties. Their commitment, like that of Rizpah, is the kind of persistence and perseverance that Jesus calls us to.

In Luke 18 Jesus tells the parable of the persistent widow. Like so many parables, this one is shocking, offering a view of widows that defies stereotypes. Though widows in the Bible are often spoken of as helpless or weak, Jesus paints a picture of a widow who is tenacious, who demands that the unjust judge grant her justice against her adversary. Some scholars even point to verse 5 as proof of this. The verse implies the judge is worried that the widow will "give him a black eye," as the literal interpretation states.[27]

Jesus points to this willful, persistent widow to teach his followers a lesson in how to engage in prayer and the pursuit of justice. "Won't God provide justice to his chosen people who cry out to him day and night?" Jesus asks. "I tell you, he will give them justice quickly" (18:7–8).

Las Madres, Rizpah, the Mothers of the Movement, and so many of our abuelitas carry the spirit of the persistent widow, a spirit we, too, should carry in our pursuit for justice.

9

Desesperación

The first time I remember Mom experiencing a low blood sugar episode was on the six-hour drive from Miami to Gainesville. My mom and stepdad, Rick, were dropping me off at college for the first time. I was a messy mix of excited and nervous. My parents, on the other hand, were anxious and sad. I'm sure I felt sad too, but not for the same reasons. I sat silent for the majority of that car ride. I mostly stared longingly out the window as the scenery shifted from the Magic City to unfamiliar wide-open fields.

As we approached the new city I'd call home, I noticed Rick peering over his right shoulder, looking at Mom with curiosity. She had been sitting quietly for far too long, wearing a distant, glazed stare. As soon as I noticed Rick's unease, I snapped my seatbelt off and poked my head between the driver and passenger seats to take a closer look. Beads of sweat had formed on Mom's forehead; her gaze had glossed over. I asked her if she was OK.

No response.

Rick's expression turned, his face tense. He asked her again if she was OK and told her to get her glucose tablets from the glove compartment.

At that moment, we realized that it had been way too long since our last meal. Mom had always been on top of her insulin injections, but she had recently switched from several injections a day to an insulin pump. And her body was still adjusting. She had no idea what Rick was talking about when he told her to grab her glucose tablets from the glove compartment.

I opened the center console and found a packet of white sugar. After tearing it open and putting it into her hand, I attempted to guide it toward her mouth. She pushed my hand away, and the contents in the packet spilled all over the passenger side of the car. I tried to explain to her that she'd go into a coma if she didn't eat the sugar, but the information wasn't registering.

She had reached the severe disorientation phase; she even looked at me and asked who I was.

That was one of the first few moments I met Mom's disability face-to-face. It was also the moment I realized how ignorant I had been of it and how it affected her body. Even as her daughter, I was unaware of the invisible burden she had carried her entire life and the lengths to which she had gone to shield me from the effects of it—which I can only imagine is added weight on her shoulders.

I knew Mom would eventually remember who I was, but I couldn't shake the eerie feeling of hearing the person who knew me the most wonder who I was.

When Abuela was first diagnosed with dementia, the fear that one day she might not know who I am gripped me, creating that sinking feeling in the pit of my stomach.

Mom ended up OK after that episode in the car. She was able to eat some sugar—thankfully before it was too late.

Mom was diagnosed with type 1 diabetes a few short years after arriving in the United States. She describes the years before her diagnosis as traumatizing because she couldn't control her excessive need to use the bathroom—a common symptom in people with diabetes due to excessive levels of sugar in the kidneys. In school, most of Mom's teachers—none of whom were Latine—denied her consistent bathroom requests, mistaking it as a behavioral issue.

To this day, Mom still struggles with being believed. Although she has spent nearly sixty years pricking and poking her skin and closely monitoring her body—how it responds to each and every thing she consumes, how her sugar levels increase and decrease at different times of the day—doctors still question her. They wonder if she's being truthful about her symptoms or whether her medical history is as accurate as she claims it to be.

This is not an isolated issue. Reports show that ethnic as well as gender bias are a common phenomenon among health-care professionals.[1] These biases increase two- and even threefold among Black people, especially women.[2]

For Mom, not being believed in school as a young girl marginalized her further, often resulting in her wetting herself in class when her teachers didn't let her use the bathroom. After several of these painfully embarrassing instances, one of Mom's teachers finally wrote a note home to let Abuela know something was up and that she should take Mom to the doctor.

Abuela hadn't noticed Mom's bathroom habits—probably because her husband had recently suffered a heart attack and his health was declining. Papi stayed in bed most days while Abuela watched after Mom, her two siblings, and the grocery store in Little Havana.

At the time, Cubans had begun taking over Miami. Those with resources—the doctors, lawyers, and such—were able to establish small businesses across Little Havana and parts of the Coral Gables area. Because of this, Abuela was able to find a Cuban clinic and visit a doctor without needing her children to translate, although this wasn't always the case. Years later, when Papi's health declined further, my aunt and uncle—still young and new to the country themselves—were tasked with the job of translating and advocating for their father.

Even so, I can only imagine what it was like for Abuela to receive the diagnosis of Mom's disease in those early years—that dizzy, disorienting feeling she must've felt upon hearing it: la diabetes.

"¿Pero solamente tiene seis años?" (But she's only six years old?)

Before having a chance to collect her thoughts, syringes, insulin bottles, and prescription slips were shoved into her hands.

I wonder if in that moment it hit her that this would be her new normal, that keeping her daughter alive would require the constant poking and pricking of her skin. I wonder if it hit Mom in that moment too.

What about my sick husband? What about money?

And food. What about food? What can she eat? What do I feed her?

When I imagine Abuela's desesperación (desperation) in this moment, I'm reminded of the Canaanite mother in Matthew 15.

Scripture includes many examples of desperate mothers—mujeres who had to make desperate decisions based on desperate circumstances.

The narrative of the Canaanite mamá (Matt. 15:21–28) isn't typically untold. However, most of the time, when people talk about it or critique it, it's often in an attempt to figure out what Jesus meant when he called the woman a "dog." Indeed, Jesus makes an alarming, seemingly out of character comment to this woman after she asks for his help: "It is not good to take the children's bread and toss it to dogs" (Matt. 15:26). Countless books and commentaries have tried to guess why Jesus would have said this, and they oftentimes engage in an apologetic defense. But one thing remains true in the telling and retelling of this passage: more often than not, this desperate, unnamed mother gets pushed to the background of her own story. Her significance is ignored, and this amplifies the marginalizing tendencies not only of the biblical text but also of critical scholarship and theological interpretation.[3]

And while I, too, am curious to understand Jesus's comment, I'm also curious to learn—and celebrate—what it is about this unnamed mamá that makes Jesus later praise her as someone who possessed great faith. Not only does Jesus engage with her (and other marginalized women, like the Samaritan woman), but their conversation is such that Jesus is challenged as much as he challenges her. "This type of dialogue holds the agency of both in a mutual and reciprocal tension, thus allowing for both to be transformed, and transforming not only each other but also the world in which they are co-creators."[4] In this theological discourse, the Canaanite mother's agency makes her someone of great faith, an abuelita theologian, a cocreator of theological insight alongside Jesus, a mujer and co-madre of wisdom and embodied knowledge.

Curious about Abuela's experience, I asked her recently how the scene at the doctor's office during that visit played out. I figured she wouldn't remember, but it was worth a try. With dementia, you never know what random memory will bubble up to the surface to greet you.

I also wanted to know what it was like for her to raise a daughter with diabetes in a new country and with limited resources. I didn't expect a thorough response, perhaps a mention about the needles, doctor's visits, or the stress of scraping together leftover change to pay for it all.

Instead, I heard something both unexpected yet oddly familiar.

"No podía comer nada." (She couldn't eat anything.)

Most of the time, Abuela's memories are jumbled together like an Ajiaco stew. Her dementia makes it hard for her to remember simple things like whether she had breakfast. Other times it's more frustrating for her, like whether her mother is still alive. "¿Y por qué no me dijeron nada?" (And why didn't you tell me anything?) she'll ask when we tell her that her mother is no longer with us. Abuela hates when she can't remember the important things. We all do.

Every once in a while, Abuela will fixate on a memory that seems to rise to the surface from the deep caverns of her mind. Sometimes these memories make us laugh; other times they make us cry. Either way, we like to think that these are raw and untempered emotions that have lain dormant for decades. These unaltered memories provide a glimpse of a life once lived. When everything else is lost, they are reminders of moments that made her *her*.

She fixates regularly on her first husband, her isla, and me in elementary school. She regularly wonders if I've had my after-school snack.

In the case of Mom's diabetes, the only thing Abuela remembers is the agony of not being able to allow her daughter to eat like everyone else. And if you're familiar at all with Latine culture, you know this makes perfect sense.

For many immigrants, food is more than just something that satisfies physical hunger. Food and the community that comes with a shared meal hold an intimate space. It is the doorway to who we are, shaping our identity and allowing us to connect with our culture.[5] For Cubans in Miami, every bite of ropa vieja (a shredded beef dish) is a taste of the motherland. Food is existence, and food is sustenance. And when you've escaped your home because of a scarcity of it, you learn to recognize how precious and how necessary—both physically and spiritually—it is for survival. "¿Ya comiste?" is more than a surface-level question about whether you've had something to eat.

"¿Ya comiste?" is a soul question. Are you satisfied? Are you filled?

As a kid, I used to roll my eyes with an exasperated "Síííí" (Yessss) every time a Cuban abuelita asked me this question. But as an adult, I get it. There are times now that even if I just had lunch, I respond from the deepest part of my spirit when I answer, "No, no comí" (No, I haven't eaten). Before I know it, a plate full of warm familiarity will be placed in front of me with a reassurance that I'm known, seen, understood, and loved. For many Latin American women, preparing food is spiritual, a labor of love, a form of embodied knowledge. I never once saw Abuela open a cookbook. In many ways, the spirit of her ancestors guided her hands in the kitchen.

At Abuela's house, preparing dinner usually began right after breakfast. The aroma would linger on for hours as Abuela chopped and seasoned—always without a recipe. She would invite me to join her, guiding my hand in slicing the onion and filling the pot of water to the perfect volume. Together we'd stare out the kitchen window at her mango and aguacate trees while arroz (rice) simmered in the pot for what seemed like days. Those hours in the kitchen with Abuela are part of what shaped me; they're the essence of abuelita theology.

"It is the slow work of making frijoles negros [black beans] while I sat alongside my abuela," explains Latina pastor Jennifer Guerra Aldana. "This theology is the aroma, the smell, the texture, the hours of labor in the kitchen. . . . It's the process by which we are formed and in which we are able to describe what God is doing among us."[6]

———

Abuela was always setting la mesa (the table)—her own mesa at that. A stainless-steel water jug served as a centerpiece; the metal utensils with black plastic handles felt too flimsy in my small hands. The wine-colored mantel draped over the glass table. Abuela's duplex is small, but la mesa always felt so big, so warm, so inviting. It's the focal point of her house right when you walk in, beckoning visitors to take a seat. After Abuela spent hours in the kitchen, familia would gather nearly every night from all over. Everyone knew there was a place at her table.

I love that Abuela set her own tables. La mesa was hers, and we were all guests. Marginalized people, especially Black, Indigenous, and other women of color, have been setting their own tables—physical and spiritual—since the beginning. Our abuelas and madrinas have been theologizing, leading us spiritually, and teaching us how to do the same. This is why I don't particularly agree with the saying "We need to make space at the table for people on the margins." People on the margins have their own tables.

However, for centuries dominant culture has insisted on building its own table alongside the marginalized, to the extent of forcing themselves into their homes and setting one right next to theirs, demanding that the marginalized get up from their own tables and sit at the table of the dominant in the name of Jesus, perhaps even claiming to do so in the name of love. But is it really loving if you force someone to leave their own table—the one they've prepared—so that they can sit at yours?

When I reflect on the ministry of Jesus, I can't help but notice that he turned table practices on their head. He did so by engaging and dignifying women of questionable purity (for example, "a sinner," Luke 7:37) in table fellowship settings, which were male-dominated and elite spaces. If he did so, then perhaps we should too.

An abuelita faith calls for the dominant culture to leave its own tables and join the marginalized at theirs. This is, in effect, a decolonized hospitality. The traditional notion of hospitality requires that we be hosts, but an abuelita theology requires that we be guests—regular guests at unfamiliar tables with only the motives of listening and learning.

Theology around la mesa in the context of an abuelita faith is a liberating praxis, a practical way to honor the tables our abuelitas have built.

We have a lot to glean from the Canaanite mother. The first important detail about her is that this mamá is nameless, something that is common for women in Scripture. Loida Martell-Otero points out that Scripture attests to the power of naming, and it is not coincidental that so many oppressed women in the Bible are nameless. In the same way, many of the abuelitas, mamás, and tías who have taught us, guided us, and inspired us also remain nameless to the wider world, often objectified or rendered invisible.[7]

However, while many of these women in Scripture are unnamed, they are far from unimportant. A few chapters earlier, we run into another nameless woman "who had been bleeding for twelve years" (Matt. 9:20). Displaying bold faith like the Canaanite mother's, she touches the edge of Jesus's cloak for a chance to be healed. Jesus notices her, and as Noemi Vega Quiñones points out in *Hermanas*, he calls her *mija* (mi hija, my daughter). "She is a woman who tells her whole truth and is a daughter belonging to the family of God." This nameless, bleeding woman, through her courage and faith, receives healing, liberation, and a new name: mija.[8]

I like to think the same is true for this Canaanite mamá. Her courage to talk back to Jesus, to claim her agency and her truth, reminds us that she isn't just a nobody in the story of Jesus. She, too, is a mija and a mamá who grants us an incredible look into abuelita faith.

Matthew 15 begins with Jesus having a discussion with legal experts about purity. They're questioning him about why he and his disciples don't partake in the ritual of washing their hands before they eat. Jesus and the legal experts go back and forth. Jesus calls them hypocrites and tells them that their lofty, robust, and seemingly theologically sound faith is empty—that they honor God with their lips but that their hearts are far from him. At the end of the scene, Jesus uses this altercation as a teaching moment for his disciples, claiming that it doesn't matter if they wash their hands, because it's not what goes into the body that contaminates but what comes out. As Jesus explains, what comes out of the mouth is from the heart.

As the narrative moves along, Jesus enters Tyre and Sidon, a region on the Mediterranean coast situated within the rural border region between Israel and Tyre. It's a non-Israelite area despised by Judeans but inhabited by a number of Israelites. Land and people are always closely interconnected, and lands have come to symbolize people and the cultural narratives ascribed to them. Therefore, as Motswana[9] postcolonial feminist scholar Musa Dube explains, geography is not just a physical body but "a page of intrinsically intertwined narratives of power and disempowerment."[10] This is important to note as the narrator tells us that "a Canaanite woman from those territories came out" to meet Jesus (Matt. 15:22). The Canaanite woman, like many Black, Indigenous, and other women of color in our midst, is characterized not by her name but by her cultural, religious, and ethnic identity as an outsider who enters a space that she shouldn't have entered.[11]

The narrator chooses to use a loaded term, *Canaanite*, to describe this woman. This is a term that not only was used to describe gentiles but was used in association with those who were conquered, colonized. Canaan is an ideologically loaded geographical marker; the name would have caused readers to recall memories of the possession of a foreign land. It was the land "flowing with milk and honey" that the Israelites were to invade and take as their own. To this end, Dube argues that characterizing this foreign woman as a *Canaanite* marks her as one who must "survive only as a colonized mind, a subjugated and domesticated subject."[12] This point is reinforced in how the disciples urge Jesus to "send her away" (Matt. 15:23) after she cries out to him for mercy.

Canaanite could have also been understood as a derogatory term, similar to a gentile being called a "dog" or a "pig," both impure animals.[13] This is striking, considering the previous controversy between Jesus and the legal experts over purity laws. Canaanites, like Samaritans, were seen as unclean by birth. By using *Canaanite* and naming the region "Tyre and Sidon," Matthew is highlighting the negative connotation of this woman's ethnicity.[14] As one scholar puts it, "An ethno-centered, urban, well-to-do predominantly Israelite community could be very threatened by persons from such a socially mixed region."[15]

Thus, the systemic oppression this mamá faces is heavy; it is based on her gender, ethnicity, and socioeconomic status. Besides being an unclean gentile, she is in a public space as a woman. She is "the poorest of the poor and most despised of the outcasts—a Gentile woman on her own before God and humankind."[16] On top of this, her daughter is suffering from demonic possession, making her doubly unclean, adding an extra dose of contamination.

While the scene is self-explanatory, there's something deeper going on. Matthew's Gospel begins with a genealogy that I don't think should be overlooked.

Here's a summary (Matt. 1:1–16, emphasis mine):

"A record of the ancestors of Jesus Christ, son of David, son of Abraham."

Matthew begins with Abraham, continues through Judah and his brothers, and then states that Judah was the father of Perez and Zerah, "whose mother was *Tamar*."

Then he continues with Hezron through Salmon, the father of Boaz, "whose mother was *Rahab*."

Then Boaz, the father of Obed, "whose mother was *Ruth*."

He then continues with Obed through King David, who is the father of Solomon, "whose mother had been the wife of Uriah (also known as *Bathsheba*)."

Matthan was the father of Jacob and Jacob of Joseph, "the husband of *Mary*—of whom Jesus was born, who is called the Christ."

Genealogies were common in the ancient world. The Bible includes these family lists in order to show where certain families came from and why they were important. But two things stick out about this genealogy: (1) it includes non-Israelites, and (2) those non-Israelites were women.

Genealogies didn't typically include women. But Matthew includes four non-Israelite women! What's more, instead of the expected ancestral mothers of the Jewish faith—Sarah, Rebecca, Rachel, and Leah—Matthew mentions (1) Tamar, the trick*star* from Genesis 38; (2) Rahab, presumed to be the prostitute from Jericho (Josh. 2; 6); (3) Ruth, the Moabite who seduces Boaz (Ruth 3); and (4) "the wife of Uriah," better known as Bathsheba, the woman King David sexually assaults (2 Sam. 11).[17]

Mentioning these (seemingly questionable) mujeres—ancestors—in Jesus's genealogy would have prompted first-century readers to pay attention. Tamar and Rahab stand out because they are believed to be Canaanite women who don't have the best reputation because they're seen as unclean and are accused of promiscuity. However, being included in the genealogy means that they are regarded as foremothers of King David, and more important, foremothers of Jesus. They are given an everlasting name as mothers of the messianic line of kings.

Thus, Matthew is starting his Gospel with a bold statement. These women represent surprise and scandal, or "holy irregularities" in God's orderly plan. They reveal sacred disruptions and discontinuities within the continuity of history. And it's the inclusion of these women in the genealogy that anticipates the "surprise and scandal" of the Canaanite woman's story.[18]

Not only is Matthew communicating the significance of this Canaanite woman's encounter through his narrative; her own words communicate surprising and scandalous truths. As she runs after Jesus, she shouts to him, highlighting her desesperación, her need, and her belief in the power of Jesus to help her. She is crying out to the point that the disciples want to be relieved from this embarrassing and persistent mamá. As I mentioned, they don't ask Jesus to help her, as is his usual practice, but instead to "send her away" (Matt. 15:23).[19]

"Show me mercy, Son of David" (Matt. 15:22), she cries. These three words offer a theological explosive. This unnamed woman acknowledges Jesus in a way that many of his own people had not yet done. "Notably, Jesus' Davidic sonship is recognized by marginal individuals rather than by the whole nation, as one would expect with regard to the long-awaited Messiah for a politically dominated people."[20]

The Canaanite mamá, like the mujeres of the genealogy, is a wise woman, courageously speaking and behaving as capable and worthy—a mujer whose strength is manifest in her persistence with Jesus.

No one would have considered this mamá a robust theologian. However, after Jesus's seemingly cruel comment toward her—"It is not good to take the children's bread and toss it to dogs"—she responds with a theological understanding so deep that Jesus couldn't refuse to show mercy: "Yes, Lord. But even the dogs eat the crumbs that fall off their masters' table" (Matt. 15:26–27).

It is likely that original readers would have connected bread to divine embodied sabiduría (Greek: *sophia*). The book of Sirach, which was included in early Jewish Wisdom literature, describes wisdom as a woman sent particularly to Israel to offer the "bread" of understanding (Sir. 15:3). Jesus and the mamá's conversation about bread also recalls the bread of the miraculous feeding found a chapter before in Matthew 14. Perhaps *bread* is used as a metaphor for what Jesus offers to the people of Israel: *Sophia*-Jesus feeds them with the bread of life and understanding, and abundantly satisfies their hunger.[21]

This mamá comprehends what so many have missed, what my abuelita and so many other unrecognized theologians understand so deeply: *food is survival and food is sustenance.* And when it comes to Jesus—the Bread of Life—there is enough food to go around for those who gather around his table.

A decolonized reading also highlights the way this Canaanite mujer redeems her native land—known as a land flowing with milk and honey—by her presence, asserting that it is rich both materially and spiritually.[22] After all, the colonized Canaanite other in this story presents a sabiduría and a theological understanding that is unparalleled. And the best part? Jesus responds to her comment with "Mujer [woman], you have great faith" (Matt. 15:28 alt.).

Her faith is a faith of survival and of persistence, an abuelita faith.

When the world overlooks this unnamed woman's understanding of who God is, when the world overlooks her wisdom and her faith because of her status and her marginalization, Jesus doesn't. Instead, he tells her, "Mujer, you have great faith." When even followers of Jesus want to send her away because they think she's unclean and a bother (Matt. 15:23), Jesus recognizes her persistence and her desperation: "Mujer, you have great faith." Up to this point, the disciples have yet to recognize such truths about Jesus. In fact, they don't recognize them until the following chapter in the book of Matthew, where Jesus asks Peter, "Who do you say that I am?" and Peter responds for the first time that he is the Christ, but only after he walks on water and witnesses two miraculous feedings. However, this woman—this nameless, marginalized, unclean mujer—articulates who Jesus is without all the background training the disciples got.

This mamá, characterized ethnically and culturally as a religious outsider, enters the theological argument (surely something that was not "her place"), turns it against itself, and achieves the well-being of her mijita, her daughter. Her disruptive entrance into theological argument is fueled by her desperation in trying to keep not just herself alive but also her daughter.[23] Ultimately, she transgresses ethnic and religious boundaries in her movement toward liberation.[24] In that, she lives out an abuelita faith, and it's that abuelita faith that Jesus commends.

⁓

Mom told me recently that as a young kid, she hid a large trash bag in her closet where she'd keep every single needle she used from her daily injections. Within months, she had hundreds of them. Mom's not sure why she kept them, stored and hidden. I wonder if for her those needles served as a visible reminder of her invisible reality that most people around her didn't understand.

In her poem "Wonder Woman," Ada Limón writes about the invisibility of her pain: strangers tell her she looks happy while she grins, shifting to her "good side."[25] She explains how other people don't understand or notice what's happening inside of her body. So she smiles, as she shifts in discomfort, keeping up the charade. "Pain, while felt fiercely, can go unnoticed not only by strangers but by friends and coworkers who may find others' discomfort uncomfortable fodder for an otherwise pleasant interaction."[26]

I told Mom recently about Abuela's response to my question concerning her diagnosis. She had a curious look at first, scanning her mind for memories. But a smile began to form as she recalled a special memory. "I didn't attend many birthday parties growing up because I couldn't eat the sweets that were usually served," she said. Her disability kept her from doing the regular things other kids did. "But I think Abuela's burden of keeping me from enjoying party food must have gotten too heavy to bear." A week before a friend's birthday party, Abuela took Mom to the doctor just to ask if she'd be able to enjoy a piece of cake. "Por favor" (Please), they begged the doctor. "We promise it'll be tiny."

Mom remembers the joy they both experienced when the doctor gave them the go-ahead.

The moment was sweet not only for Mom but also for Abuela—the news that her daughter could enjoy a treat like the rest of her peers. I wonder if it's one of those memories lodged in a crevice of her mind, waiting to bubble up to the surface at just the right moment.

10

A Divine Baile

In February 2020, about one hundred million people watched Super Bowl LIV, which took place at the Hard Rock Stadium in Miami. The half-time show was headlined by Shakira and Jennifer Lopez, two Latina women whose careers have influenced me significantly. A couple days after my tenth birthday, Jennifer Lopez (J.Lo) and Marc Anthony released their hit single, "No Me Ames." I remember how empowered I felt that year as I saved birthday money to purchase my first CD with my own money—a CD that contained only this song and its remix. I had been introduced to J.Lo two years prior when she starred in the biopic *Selena* as one of the most celebrated Latina entertainers in the early '90s.

I still remember the day Selena was shot and killed. I was young, but I remember how confusing and traumatizing it was for so many in my community. Her music had formed me from such a young age, and I was trying to understand what it meant that she was gone. The night that we watched J.Lo play Selena's life out so powerfully was unique in many ways. Mom and I had been waiting, excited for the movie to arrive at our local Blockbuster so we could cuddle in bed and watch it together. We cried uncontrollably as we watched the scene in which Selena was murdered; she was shot in real life by Yolanda Saldívar at a motel in Texas. Moments later, we were alarmed when we heard gunshots at a distance outside our window.

There had been a shooting down the street at La Vaquita, a small convenience store popular in Miami for its drive-through sales. You could pull up to any one of these convenience stores and call out to the attendant what you needed. You'd pay them, most of the time in cash, and the attendant would hand over the product, usually milk or a can of frijoles negros. Someone decided to rob La Vaquita the same night we watched the reenactment of Selena's murder—one of the first moments I began to realize that the world is really small and really large at the same time. I felt strangely connected to Selena's story that night, simply because the pop of gunshots sounded closer than they should have.

J.Lo came to represent so much for me as a fellow Caribbean Latina in the US. Her presence on TV empowered me, and her music, in English and in Spanish, made me feel seen in the multiple worlds I inhabit. Perhaps this is why I was excited as an adult to hear that she would be headlining the most widely watched show on television, representing the cultures and music that shaped me in the city that formed me.

As I watched their performance with a group of mostly seminary students and pastors on that chilly February day in Los Angeles, we cheered at the energy on that stage and danced to the Afro-Caribbean beats—the rhythms that have lived in my body, passed on to me by those whose DNA formed me.

In addition to J.Lo and Selena, the sounds of the queen of salsa, Celia Cruz, served as the soundtrack to my life growing up. Her cackling refrain of "¡Azúcar!" and her large, wide smile carried familiarity; her messages of joy and hope were favored among my people. "La vida es un carnaval" (Life is a carnival), she would famously sing.

Cruz was important for many reasons. Cruz was an Afro-Cuban born in Santos Suárez, a working-class neighborhood outside of Havana. Not only did Cruz deny her father's desire for her to abandon singing for teaching, but she rose to international fame as a Black Latina in the 1950s and 1960s, despite widespread and systemic racism and sexism. Cruz's rich and powerful voice penetrated the machismo and hypermasculine bravado of the salsa industry.

In her music, Cruz brilliantly wove together elements of classic Afro-Cuban son montuno rhythms alongside elements of guaguancó, incorporating undertones of rumba, mambo, cha-cha, guaracha, and bolero. Ethnomusicologist Michael Veal names Cruz as one of the central figures of the West African diaspora in the Caribbean who infused not only their music but a folkloric sensibility into their songs. More than a million enslaved Africans were brought to Cuba as part of the Atlantic slave trade that existed from the sixteenth to the nineteenth centuries. Because they outnumbered white settlers by the seventeenth and eighteenth centuries, Africans in the Caribbean were able to preserve their religious beliefs and musical practices.[1]

Cruz was denied permission to return to Cuba to bury her mother because she was a popular artist vocally opposed to the Cuban Revolution. She used her lyrics to tell of her pain and her own unique experiences—from the weight of her exile and longing for Cuba in "Cuando Salí de Cuba" to her experiences as an immigrant in the US in "Son Con Guaguancó." Cruz was—and still is—a source of pride for the Cuban American community. Her self-affirmations and the reclaiming of her power as a Black Latina in songs like "Bemba Colorá" will forever serve as declarations of empowerment for millions like her. Cruz made these declarations not just with her words and with sounds but by the movements of her Black body: free and gyrating on that stage—and inviting others to join along—in the ways her body was designed to by the divine.

———

Well into their old age, Abuela and Mario were part of a salsa club they attended nearly every week, spending countless hours dancing, often until the early morning. Abuela was never much of a drinker, but on those nights she'd stumble home like a teenager, giggling, intoxicated with joy, while she hung on to Mario's arm.

In many ways, el baile (dance) was Abuela's own form of embodied knowledge—the way her body knew how to move to the drumbeat, how her hips would sway, and how she and her partner knew the exact steps to take, their bodies flowing in synergy, bending and twirling in unison like flocks of birds that know the perfect moment to dip and swoop. I learned birds are not only following each other when they flock together; they know each other so well that they *anticipate* each other's moves. Perhaps the Creator made us that way too. The wisdom our bodies hold is sacred; they have a knowledge and a language of their own.

When reflecting on danza azteca (Aztecan dance), María Figueroa asks, "How does one explain that each step is a word, a syllable composing spiritual language?"[2] Our bodies can communicate with each other through salsa in ways our minds might not even understand. For many people across history, dance has been connected to the sacred, a means of embodying one's essence.[3] For many Indigenous communities, dance was a way of connecting with each other and the divine.

In fact, the Indigenous people of Mesoamerica believed that the proper way to speak of the divine was not through metaphysical or philosophical assertions but rather through flor y canto (flower and song). Today, coritos are a common way for Latina women to engage in worship. Coritos can be translated as something akin to "small choruses" of lamentation or expressions of joy. "They are testimonios [testimonies] expressed through music," explains Maldonado Pérez.[4]

Abuela was diagnosed with colon cancer when she was well into her eighties. It was a hard time for our familia, as we weren't sure she'd make it. Surviving cancer at such a vulnerable age isn't a guarantee. After one of Abuela's first chemo sessions, she walked through the door arm in arm with Mom. "Llegamos" (We've arrived), Mom said. Abuela locked eyes with me and burst into song: "¡Aleluya, gloria a Dios!" (Hallelujah, glory to God!) I'll always remember that moment. It spoke volumes to me. In her proclamation to God, I believe Abuela expressed both the depth of the hardship of beginning chemotherapy and also the gratitude and the joy of being alive another day. I wonder if she learned to use her voice this way during the decades she spent singing on the choir at church in the presence of women and men from her community, declaring in unison the goodness and greatness of the divine.

Throughout history, song and dance have oftentimes been a more effective means for our abuelitas and our ancestors to communicate the depth of their encounters with God.[5]

One of the greatest devastations of colonization is that it resulted in disembodiment. Bodies were enslaved, detached from the soul, deemed "savage," "uncivilized," "evil," "lustful." Our bodies and the songs thereof—once sacred, holders of wisdom, and masterpieces of Creator—suddenly became *things*, *objects* to be owned and controlled into submission. Throughout history, oppressed bodies have been beaten, raped, and chained—physical realities that manifest spiritually. Our songs have been silenced. When a body is physically subjugated, the soul is inevitably weakened, even destroyed. This is why the effects of slavery carry a generational trauma, and why God's heart for God's people included a *physical* freedom from bondage.

In Exodus 14, we read one of the most beloved Sunday school stories: the parting of the Red Sea. The enslaved Israelites had fled Egypt, and the Egyptian army was after them, so Moses stretched his hand over the sea, and God parted it so the Israelites could pass through on dry land. When the Egyptians tried to follow, their chariots got stuck, and the waters flowed back, killing the entire army that was after them. In response, the Israelites broke out in song and dance, thanking God for sparing their lives from those who had previously enslaved them and were out to kill them. Exodus 15 highlights this chorus of celebration, ending with the detail that "Miriam the prophet . . . took a timbrel in her hand, and all the women followed her, with timbrels and dancing" (Exod. 15:20 NIV).

The midrash (ancient Jewish commentary) affirms Miriam's righteousness in having prepared musical instruments before leaving Egypt, implying that Miriam had planned to use timbrels in dance almost intuitively, "having faith a miracle might be forthcoming."[6] Leading the women in song and dance was also understood by the midrash as a major event in Miriam's life, and this is the first song in Scripture by a woman. Judges and 1 Samuel also chronicle women going forth with music and dance to hail the returning victorious hero, which implies that this was a common role for women in ancient Israel.[7] Elsewhere in Scripture, the "joy of the Lord" is often described in expressions of song and dance, flor y canto (Pss. 30:11–12; 149:3–4; 150; Eccles. 3:4; Jer. 31:4, 12–13; Lam. 5:15). Throughout history, including the narratives detailed in Scripture, the movement of our bodies has been described as a form of celebration, a prayer of joy and gratitude to God. I believe that this is part of the reason why the body was so crucial for colonizers to suppress: to limit the expression of freedom and joy.

In this way, I see Miriam leading the Israelite community in flor y canto as a form of resistance to oppressive powers, as a response to the freedom they now have as once-subjugated bodies.

I think this is particularly poignant for Miriam, a woman. As we learn in Exodus, women were not only subjected to forced labor but raped, impregnated, and expected to deliver and nurse children to health. As women, our bodies carry life, healing, and power—perhaps this is why they are often seen as objects in need of taming and subduing.

Moments after the halftime show, one of my close friends, Esther, a fellow Cubana Americana from Miami, posted on Facebook how proud she was to be a Latina and how represented she felt. While the show wasn't perfect (for example, its lack of representation of Afro-Latine artists), many aspects of it also stirred up pride in me: the energy on that stage, the fact that my city and my culture and my songs were celebrated, and most importantly, J.Lo's and Shakira's audacity to engage their subversive messages of resistance and liberation. For one, their show was uniquely Latine, celebrating not only us but the diversity that comes with being a Latine person, leaving their mark on the most overtly US American televised sporting event. During a time when videos are going viral of Latine people being told to "go home" for speaking Spanish, having two Latina women sing and speak our language on the biggest stage of the year was in and of itself an act of subversion. Not to mention, J.Lo surprised us with a Puerto Rican flag on her tulle-and-feather cape during a "Born in the USA" medley, a message that spoke volumes to the neglect and contempt with which Puerto Rico had been treated at the time, particularly in the aftermath of Hurricane Maria, which killed thousands of people and exasperated an already strained financial situation. Lastly, the glowing cages emerging from the field—with children inside of them—at the start of "Let's Get Loud," were understood to be a way of bringing to center stage the human rights crisis at the US-Mexico border.

Esther was attacked on Facebook after posting about her pride. Many felt differently than she did about the show, claiming it was obscene and explicit. There were no sexual dances with men specifically; however, commentators—including the many opinion pieces and editorials written—fixated on the moral depravity of the outfits and suggestive body movements.

This wasn't the first time a woman of color was shamed on a Super Bowl stage. In 2004, Janet Jackson was the headliner, and she invited Justin Timberlake to be her surprise guest. Timberlake had just recently begun his solo career apart from NSYNC, and this show proved to be a big deal for him as a solo artist, as Jackson was a seasoned performer and Timberlake's career was still on the rise. The infamous "Nipplegate" incident occurred during the performance.[8]

Timberlake was to remove a part of Janet Jackson's wardrobe at the end of his routine; however, instead of removing the top part of Janet's outfit, which was intended to leave her with a red piece of lace, Timberlake accidentally ripped off the entire piece of clothing, exposing her bare breast. This incident became a huge deal, making headline news. Consequently, the FCC received more than five hundred thousand complaints, CBS was fined $550,000, and the NFL was asked to refund the $10 million they had been given by the halftime show sponsor.

After the incident, Viacom blacklisted Jackson, keeping her music videos off their properties, including MTV, VH1, and radio stations under their umbrella. CBS (broadcaster of both the Super Bowl and the Grammys) also rescinded Jackson's invitation to present the Luther Vandross tribute at the 2004 Grammys. Meanwhile, Timberlake remained McDonald's celebrity endorser despite them finding the halftime show "inappropriate." Not only did he attend the Grammys Jackson was barred from, but Timberlake also won a pair of awards. While his popularity and career continued to grow after the incident, Jackson's crumbled.[9]

The prevailing stereotype of the oversexualized Black, Brown, or Asian body is nothing new. "They go as naked as when their mothers bore them. . . . They are very well formed, with handsome bodies and good faces," wrote Christopher Columbus in his journal after his first voyage.[10] "They showed no more embarrassment than animals."[11]

What was once a way of being, of existing in the world free and without shame, quickly became inappropriate as soon as European invaders entered the scene. According to the white colonizers, the Native and Indigenous body—the Brown or Black body—was shameful, something that needed to be covered, "civilized," and "tamed." This set new standards for what was acceptable—enforcing Western modes of domesticity that erased what it perceived as moral degeneracy. This way of thinking has carried through for centuries. As historian Amy Fallas puts it, "The claims from evangelical writers and commentators about Shakira's and Jennifer Lopez's performance are a contemporary reincarnation of a very old imperial narrative."[12]

The bodies of many Latinas and other women of color have been exoticized and eroticized, robbing us of voice and power and justifying the violence done against us. And Christian spaces have only perpetuated these myths, objectifying our bodies and labeling them a temptation, as was the case in the heinous 2021 Atlanta shootings in which Asian women were targeted. Thus, we are forced to accept projections of lustful desires that result in shame and guilt.[13]

Another centuries-old trope is that the burden of lust always falls on women. This is a burden that destroys us not only physically but morally too. I wonder, What if Christian men and women retrained their minds to appreciate the strength and beauty in a woman's body without seeing it merely as a cause to stumble, or worse yet, as a one-dimensional object suitable simply for pleasure or procreation? What's interesting is that according to Jesus in Matthew 5:28–29, the burden of stumbling ought to fall on men, not women. Jesus told men that if they looked at a woman lustfully, they were to rip their eye out and throw it away.

Perhaps the problem doesn't lie in individual women dancing, moving their bodies, engaging in their traditions; perhaps the problem lies in the system that hypersexualized them and deemed them inappropriate simply for existing and moving the ways that they do.

I wonder if Jesus thought it was the system that needed fixing too. Perhaps this is why when he was questioned by the religious elite about whether to stone the woman accused of adultery, Jesus urged those without sin to throw the first stone. When they all walked away, he looked at the woman and asked, "Has anyone condemned you?" "No," she said. "Neither do I," he replied (John 8:10–11). "Jesus places his authority to forgive and to offer freedom over against the religious establishment's determination of the categories of life and death," argues Gail O'Day.[14] Jesus attacks what needs to be changed—the system—so that men and women can live new lives in a new age.[15]

It's not lost on me that many of the same people who shared this level of public outrage, disappointment, or disgust at J.Lo and Shakira are also the same people who were silent at the news of seven hundred cases of sexual abuse reported in the SBC. This reality pains me. I wonder what our world would look like if sexual abuse in the church were more infuriating to Christians—particularly Christian women—than Latinas dancing on stage.

As with most injustices in our society, it's easier to blame the individual than the system because blaming the system means we all play a part in upholding it and are thus accountable. Ephesians 6:12 says that we are fighting "against rulers, authorities, forces of cosmic darkness, and spiritual powers of evil in the heavens." Part of these invisible forces are systems that dehumanize, subjugate, and oppress—systems that keep abusive men in power while silencing their victims.

Argentinean scholar Marcella Althaus-Reid poignantly asks, "Where would God be in a salsa bar?"[16] For her, bodies add theological insights to the quest for love and for truth, but many theologians fail to look for God in these spaces.[17] But the more I read about the Jesus in the Gospels, the fully embodied God who was often found in unconventional places, the more I believe not only that he would be in a salsa bar, dipping and swirling us as we engaged in a divine baile with him, but that La Espíritu Santa herself *is* the un-dos-tres-bachata[18]—the one who created our bodies in motion, who urges us to worship in song and dance like Miriam, who wants us to bring our full selves and the expressions thereof to the table, or the dance floor.

The memories of my time at the first seminary I attended are marked with both hardship and growth, beauty and pain. But some of my favorite—and more helpful—memories are with my friend and roommate at the time, Quaneisha. Quaneisha is a Black woman from the South who has a love for dancing salsa, and when she found out that I was Cuban, she quickly made plans for me to visit different salsa clubs and bars with her. Quaneisha and I were among the few women of color on campus. Every once in a while, after long weeks of navigating life and theology in a white man's world, we'd put on our dancing shoes, head to a salsa bar, and set our bodies free, twirling and spinning and laughing the night away. Those nights were abundantly healing for me. I didn't have the language to express why back then, but my body knew.

Our bodies carry sacred wisdom. Traditionally, however, instead of being taught to listen to, care for, and love our bodies as temples of divinity and life, we are taught to disconnect from them. As author and therapist K. J. Ramsey writes, "We're a people formed around worshipping the God who so loved us embodied people that he became one of us, but we treat our bodies with suspicion and contempt instead of sacred awe."[19] It's no wonder that trauma specialists and therapists suggest befriending our bodies as a way of not only healing but claiming our agency.[20] I think nights spent on the dance floor with Mario served those purposes for Abuela as she befriended and learned to love the movements of her own body.

Our bodies tell stories. Stories about ourselves and even stories about the divine. May we learn to listen.

One story that my body often tells is the story of being in between worlds.

Mexican American theologian Virgilio Elizondo writes about living in between two worlds, that his entire life he felt pulled in two directions: the US way of life and the Mexican way of life. "Sometimes I felt the pull would be so great that it would rip me apart. But I could not run away either to the US or to Mexico, for both were as much a part of me as I was a part of them."[21] I think many of us feel like we need to fit on either end of that pull, but what if, as Elizondo and many others ask, this "between" space is a frontier zone? A dance floor that brings together two worlds, two languages, two ways of life—an interstitial space where life's greatest lessons are learned, where God is most present?

In decolonized conversations, the interstitial space is also referred to as the liminal space, a site of identity formation for many marginalized communities. It is a space of "deformation, reformation and transformation," explains African American biblical scholar Lynn St. Clair Darden. "The middle space is not a space of separation that produces privilege, but a space of mutual lingering and active interaction between cultures."[22] I think what makes this space so heavy is that for many, it's the space between the colonizer and the colonized. "[It's] the interstitial space in which both conflict and mutual assimilation occur when two cultures encounter each other."[23]

I think many voices are often lost in this interstitial space. The colonial binary, whether liberal or progressive, left or right, over-looks this middle space between colonized and colonizer, where Western religion, African spirituality, and Indigenous tradition often meet. This is a space where I believe abuelita theology exists. Now, I know this space was created by a forced mixing, a painful reality—so I don't wish to romanticize it, only reclaim it. Like Anzaldúa says, "The mixture of bloods and affinities, rather than confusing or unbalancing me, has forced me to achieve a kind of equilibrium. Both cultures deny me a place in *their* universe. Between them and among others, I build my own universe, *El Mundo Zurdo*. I belong to myself and not to any one people."[24]

For women specifically, it's more than a crossing of two worlds or two borders; it's a crossing of multiple worlds and borders, an existence in many worlds that we inhabit because of our gender, sexuality, color, class, personality, spirituality, and lived experiences.[25] While this space is confusing, perhaps even intimidating for the dominant culture, I wonder, What if there's freedom to dance, to engage in a divine baile in this space? The Wild Child of the Trinity, her presencia (presence) as intimate and native as God and human on the dance floor of the garden of Eden.

Whiteness, patriarchy, and colonial ideology have tried to fragment us into pieces they can understand and tame, but what if we existed, whole and free, in the full complexity of who we are? As a Cuban with Spanish, Taíno, and African ancestry; a US American; a mujer; an hija; a co-madre; a Christian—Catholic and Protestant—I dance in between worlds in the interstitial space where Miriam danced, the space between Egypt and the promised land.

11

Madre of Exile

Abuela still has a 3D portrait of white Jesus hanging over her bed. Jesus's porcelain face is carved several inches deep, making the portrait look more like a sculpture with a golden frame, one that shifts depending on the angle you look at it. In the boredom of childhood, I'd often spend hours moving from side to side as I stared, wondering if I'd catch something offbeat—a wink perhaps, or a smile. There's also a statue of Mary with baby Jesus by the TV and another framed image of the pair on the adjacent wall. One day I asked Abuela why she had so many symbols in the room. "Nos protegen mientra dormimos" (They protect us while we sleep), she said behind a slight grin.

On weekends we'd often take trips to visit Abuela's cousin Rosel. As a little girl, I always felt uncomfortable visiting Rosel's family because of the four-foot statue of San Lazaro that towered above me on their front lawn. Lazarus's open wounds and the dogs licking his sores troubled me. I didn't understand what it meant back then, that it was recalling the story Jesus told of the poor man Lazarus who sits outside the gate of a rich man, hungry, longing to eat what falls from his table. The rich man ignores Lazarus's presence; only the dogs who lick his wounds pay attention to him. Eventually, Lazarus, with all his sores, is let into heaven. The tables turn, and the rich man now becomes the one begging Lazarus for a drink of water while he burns in hell.

It's a powerful and shocking parable, one of those that makes us so uncomfortable that we try to deflect, use it to focus on constructing a theory of the afterlife instead of the consequences of overlooking the poor. But while the privileged are using this story to argue about whether those in heaven can actually have conversations with those in hell, the poor are identifying with Lazarus as a symbol of God's miracles and healing, as a reminder that God cares for the forgotten, the social outsiders whose wounds offend and disgust.

San Lazaro is a favored saint for mi gente Cubano. He serves as a symbol of the clash between oppressor and oppressed: an image of liberation birthed from a complex and complicated history. Most of the popular Catholic symbols represent a mix of the traditional Iberian Catholicism of the colonizers and the spirituality enslaved people brought with them when they were forced out of Africa.

Mi gente are people who live in a perpetual exile. In fact, Cuban theologians, among others, have named the immigration of Cubans to the US after the revolution "el exilio" (the exile). El exilio shapes and names the collective identity of the Cuban diaspora in a way similar to that of the Israelites when they left Egypt—or more specifically, when they were exiled to Babylon after the destruction of Jerusalem and the temple, which marked the end of the Jews' political sovereignty and the cessation of the Davidic monarchy in 586 BCE. It is the place from which our identity is constructed. But what strikes me about a perpetual exile in Scripture is the notion of waiting, hoping to return to the—to *a*—promised land.

While the majority of Cubans see the US as a salvific place of refuge, many fail to understand that the US bears much of the responsibility for their displacement—a common narrative in Latin American history. As Cuban theologian Justo González explains, the US, the land of our refuge, is also the land that created our need for exile. Political exiles discover the complicity of North American vested interests in the events that lead to their need to abandon their countries. Economic exiles eventually learn that the poverty of their native lands is the result of the wealth of their adoptive lands.[1] This is true for most of Latin America; our people have endured exploitation first by Western Europeans and then by the very country we now call home.

When I asked Abuela what it was like to leave Cuba, she said that she always intended to go back. Many on the island buried their jewelry and belongings, drawing maps on napkins that they kept in their pockets when they left. They envisioned a world in which they'd be able to return to their homes and the holes they dug in their gardens. They never got that. Many still live in waiting.

For Cubans, el exilio is more than a geographic separation; it encompasses disconnection, existing in a reality different from what they long for: la patria (the homeland). In Miami, the longing for Cuba, or the "rhetoric of return," has been what unifies us.[2] I feel this when I walk the streets of Miami, pop into the ventanitas (small windows) found in the corner strip malls where you order your cafecitos and pastelitos.

I felt drawn to the biblical notion of exile even before I learned how the struggles and yearnings of the Israelites intersect with my people and before I was encouraged to bring my own history into dialogue with theirs. Perhaps it was born out of this longing of a land not my own—the longing that was formed in me since I could remember. Images and songs, slang and food, they have formed me since my time in the womb. Perhaps it is the deep tethering that we experience as humans, how we are never disconnected from our ancestors and our land, no matter how far we may be removed.

Because one's land is that which gives life and shapes identity, a loss of it can often translate to homelessness and even orphanhood. Many Indigenous communities across the Americas have felt this, particularly colonized communities whose identities have been stolen from them. Oscar García-Johnson explains that "a deep sense of orphanhood [had] a traumatic effect among invaded communities that became, in a matter of years, a commodity of a foreign empire."[3] This inflicts the colonial wound. Decolonizing thinker Walter Mignolo explains that the colonial wound is where "the first world" and "the third world" collide and bleed.[4]

The colonial wound represents both the damage inflicted by hegemonic powers on oppressed peoples and their ongoing internalization and reproduction of the dehumanizing narratives. "That is why the feeling of 'orphanhood' is a constant background of our political endeavors and our personal conflicts."[5]

We are a people wounded by displacement. Because of this I often wonder, How do people create a new identity in a new place without losing their connection to the old? From el exilio we are forced to reconstruct our identities in order to not only survive but live out God's desire that we thrive.

For many Cubans, La Virgen de Caridad del Cobre, the Cuban Mary, has been most important for our collective identity, both on the island and in the diaspora. What makes her so important, however, is that she represents the Afro-Cuban roots of Cuban identity and religiosity that are often silenced or ignored.

Devotion to La Caridad began in el Oriente (the easternmost province of Cuba) in the seventeenth century among a community of slaves and continued to grow over the years. The earliest account of her appearance dates back to 1687, when an African slave named Juan Moreno and two other Indigenous brothers found her statue floating on the Bay of Nipe. By appearing to a slave and two Indigenous Cubans (subordinates to the colonial order), La Caridad upset the social order of her era.[6]

However, it wasn't until the wars for independence from Spain in the nineteenth century that La Caridad became decisively the way that Cubans imagined themselves as a nation. Throughout their battles for independence, clergy who had sided with revolutionaries, along with los mambises (Creole insurgents), appealed to the Virgin. Many of those who went off to fight wore images of La Caridad on their uniforms. Mothers, daughters, and sisters who waited for los mambises to return from battle also petitioned her on the soldiers' behalf. By the time the Spanish had been defeated, the American occupying government had departed, and an independent Cuban republic had been established, La Caridad had become "La Virgen Mambisa." She had become the rebel Virgin, the patriot Virgin, the national Virgin. She had become a symbol of liberation for the people.[7]

Mary took on additional meanings throughout the centuries. While traditional Roman Catholicism in Cuba still represented the oppressive colonial powers of Spain later on, many Cubans, including slaves, found comfort and liberation through the practices of "popular Catholicism" practiced mostly by residents who lived in el campo, far from church and any opportunity to make it to mass. This "popular Catholicism" was a blend of African spirituality and traditional Catholicism and was a common practice for many people on the island, leading to a strong spirituality and religion birthed in the home, which continued throughout exile.

Religion birthed in the home is common for many minoritized communities. For immigrants specifically, constructing and negotiating their identity happens in a variety of ways in the diaspora. For example, many retain their language, food, and music. Many also turn to religion to make sense of themselves as a displaced people.[8] Roman Catholic and Cuban theologian Alex García-Rivera notes the importance of symbols in the popular Catholicism of the Latin American church: "The experience of the ecclesial tradition of the Latin church of the Americas is the experience of a Community of the Beautiful. It is the experience of Beauty in the furnace of a violent history."[9] To this end, symbols act as homing devices. Jacqueline Hidalgo explains that religious symbols (like Mary) for some communities can be about making, contesting, and reshaping place rather than just navigating a world neatly divided between sacred and profane.[10]

Growing up I loved spending time with one of Abuela's closest friends from Cuba, Yami. I always had a blast with Yami. She taught me how to make tiny chairs and couches and homes from pieces of cardboard. We'd spend hours in the kitchen rolling buñuelos (fritters) into figure eights to hand out to friends and family. I'd often stay with her in her small apartment in the heart of Little Havana. I loved doing so because she didn't have a car, so we'd take the bus and venture through the city, stopping at corner bodegas to grab a croqueta (croquette) and a lottery ticket. I loved scratching the silver surface, excited for what we might win. One time we won ten dollars, and we jumped up and down with excitement: "¡Ganamos, Katy!" (We won, Katy!), she exclaimed.

We'd walk down the street of Calle Ocho, hand in hand, as she'd say hello to the local store owners blasting salsa from their small speakers. Yami had a love for la vida, for life, that was contagious; her laugh was loud, more like a shriek. She was vulgar, her jokes often about bodily fluids and how funny everyone around her looked. But no one seemed to mind her raunchiness; even Abuela would laugh and roll her eyes. Yami was a woman sin vergüenza, without shame. *Vergüenza* is often used in a derogatory sense in Spanish, but I wonder if it could be reclaimed—if living without shame in our communities can become something to be proud of.

Yami's reality was complicated. She was a poor, brown-skinned woman who held both a passion and a love for life, as well as a deep well of pain and sorrow. Yami's son had come out as gay in the late '80s and was a victim of HIV. This reality made him tainted to the outside world, particularly because of the machismo that infects many Cuban men, who assert their dominance over women, LGBTQIA+ persons, and anyone who doesn't show the typical macho bravado that is expected. Like Lazaro, Yami's son was seen as a man with sores, unworthy of love. Sometimes, when life slowed down and things were quiet in the house, I could sense Yami's pain. She loved and accepted her son, but in a culture where toxic masculinity is central, she worried for his safety and how he was treated.

Some of my most vivid memories with Yami include us sitting cross-legged in front of the altar she made at her house; it was decorated with flowers and candles, which she lit to los santos, the saints. Yami regularly petitioned los santos for her son's protection and that those lottery tickets would bring forth a miracle. She asked for the money not to get herself a decent apartment but to help her son with his treatment. I didn't understand the depths of her petitions to La Caridad or to San Lazaro, but I knew they were important. And as I sat there next to Yami as she held her rosary and whispered the Padre Nuestro (the Our Father prayer), I knew it was a sacred space, that God was listening to her, to our petitions.

What pains me is how I was taught to distrust these moments once I was introduced to evangelicalism, particularly because of the way that I began to see these symbols or rituals. They went from being symbols of familiarity and spirituality within my culture, to symbols of evil and signs that the immigrant community of which I had been a part needed to be saved, rescued from its so-called paganism. I realize now that this has less to do with a marginalized community's lack of faith than it does with dominant culture's control of what are legitimate expressions of "true spirituality" or even what makes someone worthy enough to worship. According to many parts of the dominant culture, not only would Yami's spirituality be seen as wrong or false, but the details of her life would exclude her from participating in the body of Christ.

Yami, like many other poor women, had been caught in a web of power. Her son was conceived in an affair she had with the owner of the house it was her job to clean. While Yami was working as a housekeeper for a wealthy family, the husband took interest in her, eventually pursuing her, impregnating her, then paying her off to stay silent—not unlike King David using his own power and authority to invite another man's wife into his bed and then doing what he could so that no one found out. This narrative is surprisingly common; many poor women fall victim to "indecency" due to the unequal power relations they often exist within, leaving them with very little room for negotiation.

In her book *Indecent Theology*, Marcella Althaus-Reid criticizes dominant Christianity's—even liberation theology's—tendencies to romanticize the poor. When we imagine the poor, we tend to essentialize them. "Who do we think the poor are?" Althaus-Reid asks. "Virgin Marys coming from heaven with a rosary in their hands?"[11] A peasant Mary is often portrayed simply dressed with a clean, smiling face. But is this reality? Althaus-Reid reminds us that the young, poor women from the villas miserias (slums) often wear dirty faces and short, ill-fitting dresses. Their bodies often tell stories of sexual abuse and harassment. Poor women are seldom virgins or women committed to a so-called holy life. Poverty forces people to do what Christians would consider indecent and questionable things.[12]

I wonder, Are poor women's expressions of spirituality considered legitimate worship only if they fall within the parameters of "decency"—only if they're not forced into sex work or into relationships with married men?

The poor woman highlighted in many of our churches "was never the poor woman who was fighting to be ordained as a minister in her church, nor the poor mother trying to get an abortion or struggling, not against capitalism, but against abusive Christian men in her family."[13]

Yami was committed to her faith, but she was also committed to her survival. Exile forces this reality on many people; however, Yami found strength in her prayers and petitions. And perhaps she made a sacred space within her home because the church wouldn't make a place for her. Perhaps she felt she could engage in worship only by herself in her small apartment in Little Havana because even the liberationists, who care about the poor, didn't care about *her kind* of poor.

Was God not present with her? Did God abandon her because she didn't fit prevailing notions of womanhood—the poor mother, the "decent virgin"? Is the poor woman who is highlighted in many of our churches and theologies considered legitimate only if she's not caught in patriarchal webs of power and abuse, impregnated, and the mother of a gay son?

───────

What I find complicated, like the lived experiences of many of the abuelitas around us, is the Catch-22 of many of their, of our, cherished symbols.

The veneration of Mary was introduced in the imperial conquest in Latin America alongside the introduction of the cross of Jesus. While the veneration of Mary has been around since the second century, it grew in popularity among the conquered peoples of Latin America, with many women and men taking to Mariology as a serious part of their faith practice.

Colonization began to convince Latin American women that in order to have value, they must subscribe to Western ideals like that of the "good" daughter, mother, and wife, according to European standards. And like most other thinking, this was constructed around a binary. For women, this dichotomy was that of virgin or temptress—no in between, no nuance.[14] Soon, Mary became for many Latin American women a sort of "quasi-woman," a mythical image with no connection to the lived experiences of marginalized women. Thus, some argue that patriarchy made the symbol of Mary into a machine that processes multiple *othernesses* and oppression.[15]

Historically, Mary has been upheld as the ideal woman, her characteristics and attributes unattainable by most. For example, she is often seen as a perpetual virgin and her self-sacrifice as often devoid of agency. In her domestication, she is used as a way to silence women, particularly Latin American women whose spirituality has been formed on the heels of Spanish colonization. I wonder, Has the Marian image that no "ordinary" woman can identify with ultimately shamed us for existing as we are?

I ask these questions because I want to be honest about our abuelitas and the faith they pass on to us. I never want to essentialize the reality: just as our abuelas have lived lives of resistance, have enriched us with their wisdom, they have also in many ways perpetuated these unattainable images. The effects of colonialism are such that many of our abuelas have upheld the Western ideal that a women's life has value only if it exists to serve their husbands. This is the complicated reality of our abuelas; they exist in an in-between space where everyday life is lived—where we both resist and participate in systems of oppression. This is due, in part, to the fact that their first priority is to survive.

Perhaps Yami got tangled up in a web of power and abuse because she had no choice—if she lost her job, then she'd lose her livelihood and home. Maybe it wasn't safe for her to say no— perhaps the man engaging with her was abusive.

Survival, especially within exile, makes you do things you never thought you'd do.

What makes the character of Mary complicated, like many other women in Scripture, is how she, too, can exist in this in between, how she can be used as a symbol of both oppression and liberation. This is true not only of Mary but of Scripture as a whole. The Bible has been used to justify all sorts of evils. It has also been used to liberate.

For me, Mary played an interesting role. I grew up with a sense of awe at the idea of a miraculous God, at how the divine can communicate with us so powerfully. Watching Telemundo with Abuela before bed meant that apparitions of La Caridad flooded headlines regularly. Nearly every night we'd come across a news special of a new image of Mary appearing to someone in the community: a Mary-shaped water stain on the side of the house, her image burned on a piece of toast. My entire childhood, I was both amazed and terrified that one day Mary would appear to me. I didn't know what it meant, but I knew it would be a great honor. I learned early on that God communicates to God's people, even through the most miraculous and ridiculous of ways. And for me, that was strangely comforting.

Years later, my newfound Protestant faith made me question not only the Telemundo headlines but the fact that God would speak to a marginalized community through Jesus's own marginalized mother. I realize now how important these symbols are to a people that feels displaced or often forgotten. Perhaps they don't carry as much weight to the privileged, but to women like Yami, those symbols help keep them alive. They are tangible images of hope, of who they are as children of a miraculous God who tends to the sores of the sick. This is where Mary, in her interstitial space, can also be an image of liberation, as many Protestants have embraced more and more in recent years.

Part of what makes Mary a symbol of liberation is her powerful Magnificat, or what some refer to as her "war cry," found in Luke

1:46–55. Mary's war cry is an expression of a revolutionary transformation of an unjust social order, and an overturning of power dynamics.

In the Magnificat, Mary tells of God defeating the oppressors, and she does so as a girl not yet married. This means that her pregnancy does not follow from the proper role of women, putting her in danger as someone who has been making her own choices about her body and sexuality without regard for her future husband. In Luke, Joseph is not consulted; thus the decision to have the redemptive child is between Mary and God.[16] This powerful detail speaks to a sacred reclaiming of Mary's own body in one of the most personal and intimate ways possible. As Esau McCaulley points out, the Spirit of God knit together the hope of the world in Mary's womb.[17]

Mary's war cry is one of justice, calling forth God's liberating revolution. Her cry of justice and liberation is one that announces the inauguration of a new kingdom, one that stands in contrast to the kingdoms of oppression and exploitation. "Mary is the patron saint of faithful activists who give their very bodies as witnesses to God's saving work."[18] In doing so, she calls forth both a tearing down and a rebuilding—a scattering of the proud and a lifting up of the lowly (Luke 1:51–52).

Mary becomes both subject and object of this liberating action, making it possible through her act of faith. In turn, she embodies and personifies the oppressed and subjugated people who are being liberated and exalted through God's redemptive power. As a woman, specifically a woman from among the poorer classes of a colonized people under the mighty empire of Rome, Mary represents many of our abuelitas who are to be lifted up and filled with good things in the messianic revolution.[19]

A theology of abuelitas comes alive from the pages of Scripture—from the womb of our ancestor and co-madre Mary—and it continues through the millions of immigrant daughters who carry the baton today.

My story is shaped by physical and spiritual exile. I think many of our stories are. In one way or another, they're made up of the periods that define our leaving one place—one way of being, one way of knowing—and going to another. Sometimes we experience exile from the religion or ideology of our upbringing, our cultures. Even those of us who are minoritized journey away from things that hurt us and stifle us, like machismo, a dictator god, or a militarized Christianity. This, too, marks our displacement, as we journey into tierra desconocida (unknown land).[20] I find displacement to be a spiritual phenomenon. How does one not feel at home in the only place they've ever called home?

For me, exile describes the nepantla journey. It is an unstable, unpredictable space, where there is loss and there is gain. It is also a transformative space.

Indeed, exile is a complex way of life, always lingering in our psyches. But I often wonder how it became a place of shame. Why have we let dominant culture victimize us in our in betweenness? Why do many of us feel bad, less-than, plagued by it? Has dominant culture so convinced us that permanency—in location, in belief—is somehow holy?

I wonder, What if this exiled identity is an identity in which we are most alive? I often think of all that happened for the Israelites in exile, how God was so intimately acquainted with God's people. What if instead of being ni de aquí ni de allá (neither from here nor from there), we are *de aquí y de allá* (from here and from there).

Our histories are complicated, our identities complex. This reality means that our very existence as people of dos mundos (two worlds) is one that resists dominant Western culture's preference that we fit into colonial dichotomies. The binary of Western culture has simplified our identities, made us into a one-dimensional people, and destroyed what makes us complex, like they've done with the divine. But what if our in betweenness is our superpower, where the Wild Child of the Trinity is free to roam and move sin fronteras (without borders)?

I think this resists the lie that Western Christianity has often perpetuated, the lie that reality is dualistic, that everything is black or white, that faith is as simple as pointing out what is "sin" and what is not. I think this is why the Bible is so confusing for so many Christians. Western ideology has taught us to look for dualities in a book that never meant to hold them. Instead, the Bible's narratives are messy and multilayered, its pages replete with characters who trick men into sleeping with them, who disobey authority, who lie, and even who steal and yet are still called "blessed" by God. Perhaps recognizing the complexity of the human experience within the stories of Scripture can shift how we see and engage with the other. This is part of the story that Mary tells too. Throughout the centuries, her story represents the interstitial space many of our abuelas inhabit: that space between Mary the liberator and Mary the symbol of oppression.

We tell these stories because they are the stories of God existing in the gray with God's people, of God journeying alongside them in the messiness of what it means to be human, of what it means to survive—and even attempt to thrive—in the midst of oppressive empires, in exile, in between two worlds.

12

Resolviendo in La Lucha

I often wonder when it hit Abuela that she would never go back to her isla—when she realized she wouldn't ever again feel its earth beneath her, its dirt between her fingertips. Did it hit her after she buried her husband 180 miles from home, across the Atlantic Ocean? As the soil trickled over the casket, did she imagine it was the same soil that once gave life to her mangoes and aguacates on the island?

I wasn't there when Papi was buried, of course. But I was present for Mario's burial. I still remember her shrieks as Mario's body was lowered into the ground. She tried to get up from her wheelchair, allowing the casket to break her fall: "¡Ay, ay, ay, mi amor!" I remember the white handkerchief she held over her mouth.

The last thing I recall is her kissing a rose before dropping it in the cold dark pit. I thought, *Now what? Now we're just supposed to go home?*

Even when tragedy happens, we keep going. We keep living. We keep getting by. We keep waking up and making it through another day. We resolvemos and keep resolviendo the way Abuela did after she buried her first and then second husband.

The term *resolviendo* has been used in Cuba to describe the Cubans' situation since the early 1990s, when the country began to suffer the economic consequences of the fall of the socialist countries from which its basic support came.[1] Around this time, the government announced a series of restrictions on things like food, medical supplies, and gasoline—forcing Cubans to create new economic opportunities. This created the context for Cubans to resolver, to struggle to survive. Latina theologian Cristina García-Alfonso defines *resolviendo* as la lucha of survival in which powerless people find power and agency to face their daily lives.[2] It refers to the process of people getting what they need, not for the long term or the future but for the day at hand—like the Lord's Prayer, which says, "Padre nuestro [Our Father], give us today our daily bread"—or what we need to resolver. When the disciples asked Jesus how to pray, perhaps he knew that this would be the reality of most peoples of the world: figuring out how to get by day by day. Most who embraced his message were those for whom resolviendo was their way of life.

For Cubans on the island, *resolver* covers a range of activities, including bartering, planting vegetables in their gardens, and keeping chickens in the backyard. To resolver is also to live an embodied existence, to rely on the land, the gifts of the earth, and its animal life too. Those who live their lives resolviendo understand that the struggle to survive is not an individual or isolated task but a communal experience that involves all people, particularly those in the community.[3] Resolviendo is a way of life for the majority of the world, for women in particular, both in the present and in the past.

Have you ever heard of Mahlah, Noah, Hoglah, Milcah, and Tirzah? I won't be surprised if you haven't. The first time I learned their story, I was a few years into my seminary education. Not only had I sat through countless hours of Bible teaching and sermons on the Old Testament, but I had also taken entire classes on the Hebrew Bible and still had never learned the importance of their story—how they fought for justice and how God honored their demands. While most people know and refer to them as the daughters of Zelophehad, I resist the notion to reduce them to "the daughters of . . ." They are not nameless or forgotten. So we say their names: Mahlah, Noah, Hoglah, Milcah, and Tirzah.

Mahlah, Noah, Hoglah, Milcah, and Tirzah are first introduced in Numbers 26 and are mentioned in *five* different places in the Bible. The only other people mentioned so many times across books in the Hebrew Scriptures are Miriam and Moses. The story follows the second census of the people and God's instructions to Moses about how the promised land was to be distributed among the families of the second generation. However, because God told Moses to use the census to distribute land according to paternal tribal affiliation, only males were entitled to inherit the land. Because their father had died and they were without husbands or brothers, the patriarchal system of kinship that Moses was using to allocate land excluded Mahlah, Noah, Hoglah, Milcah, and Tirzah—and probably other women who were without men in their lives—from receiving a cut.[4]

After arriving from Cuba, Abuela, too, dealt with the pangs of patriarchy and, more specifically, machismo with regard to ownership of property. While still in Cuba, Papi and other men in the family worked as carniceros (butchers) in their local supermarket. During the first year Papi was in the US, before his wife and children arrived, he was able to land a similar job at a local grocery store, as did the other carniceros in the family. After several years, a few of them were able to save enough money to purchase a small grocery store together in Little Havana.

Mom was young, but she remembers how Abuela and Papi poured their heart and soul into that store after they arrived.

It had two cash registers on each side, a couple aisles of food, a fruit stand, a carnicería (butcher shop), and a small cafeteria where they sold pastelitos and cafecitos. The store was divided into sections; each owner owned a small part. Abuela worked the register, and Mom packed bags.

As Papi became sicker, Abuela found herself spending more time at the store, working opening and closing shifts, trying to keep up with her and her husband's workloads. Mom recalls that she was barely home, spending the majority of her day trying to make ends meet. When she got home, taking care of Papi was her priority.

We aren't sure when the other store owners—members of their own family—began to devise a plan to take Papi and Abuela's portion of the store, but as soon as he died, they took action, using his death as an opportunity to push Abuela out of the business. This grocery store had been my family's livelihood, and although Abuela's passion had been sewing, she fell in love with the cash registers, the community, the families that would linger in the cafeteria. The grocery store had become a safe space, a piece of home where the outside world ceased to exist. I often wonder if Abuela lost herself in the grocery store because it lent her a sense of familiarity after leaving the motherland.

My family uses words and phrases like *torture* and *made her life a living hell* to describe what Abuela went through. "They did horrible things and said horrible things to her," Mom recalls. They wanted the store all to themselves, and now that Papi was gone, they saw a widow, a vulnerable woman without a man to protect her. Never mind all she had worked prior to and during his sickness.

Not only did Abuela have to say goodbye to Papi so soon after moving to the States, but she had to fight tooth and nail in the midst of her grief to preserve what little she had left of community, of his memory, and of their financial stability. Even at a young age, Mom felt Abuela's agony as she witnessed how hard she fought. The men were ruthless, as are the effects of patriarchy, of machismo. It looks out only for its own.

After we find out they are cut out from receiving land, we don't hear from Mahlah, Noah, Hoglah, Milcah, and Tirzah again until the beginning of Numbers 27, which leaves to the imagination envisioning the sisters deliberating the inequality of the land distribution system. I wonder, What were their conversations like as they decided that enough was enough, as so many other women did and continue to do after them?

After they are reintroduced in Numbers 27, the text says they "came forward," a detail that assumes their agency. Their timing, according to the narrative, seems deliberate, as it is at the end of the land distribution but before dispersal of the leaders.[5] Next, "they stood before Moses, Eleazer the priest, the chiefs, and the entire community at the entrance of the meeting tent" (v. 2). The narrative describes Mahlah, Noah, Hoglah, Milcah, and Tirzah taking action, placing their bodies in front of Moses, the priests, and the entire community. In fact, by placing their bodies in front of the entrance of the meeting tent, they were taking the intermediary position usually taken by Moses[6]—a bold and audacious move. After positioning themselves, the sisters make their argument, emphasizing their father's lack of male offspring and clearing his name from those "who gathered against the LORD" (v. 3). The last thing they tell Moses is "Give us property among our father's brothers" (v. 4).

They don't ask; they demand, as is demonstrated by the imperative (command) verb form in the text.[7]

I find this act incredibly daring. Mahlah, Noah, Milcah, Hoglah, and Tirzah not only come forward to speak personally, but they do so in front of the community. What makes their interaction with Moses so daring is that they question not only Moses's opinion but also a direct decree from God, pushing that a divine instruction be revised. How will God or God's representative respond? I imagine the community mumbling among one another. Were they surprised by the sisters' boldness? Were they inspired? I imagine some in the crowd feeling frustrated: *Who do they think they are?* Did some think they were being divisive, as many churchgoers nowadays accuse women of when they speak up or advocate for themselves?

Moses brings their case before God.

I envision the rustle in the crowd, the tension in the air as the women approach and as everyone waits for the verdict to be announced.

God answers, "Zelophehad's daughters are right in what they are saying. By all means, give them property as an inheritance among their father's brothers. Hand over their father's inheritance to them" (Num. 27:6–7).

God vindicates Mahlah, Noah, Hoglah, Milcah, and Tirzah!

Their assertiveness in standing up against unjust laws is matched by God's response: "[They] are right. . . . Give them property." What God does next is one of my favorite moves in the Bible; God changes the law, adjusts it to include women in future inheritances. "Speak to the Israelites and say: If a man dies and doesn't have a son, you must hand his inheritance over to his daughters" (Num. 27:8). The image of God's mind changing in response to the sisters' request is not lost on me; it is profound.

God listened to the cries of the women and took action on their behalf. When those who are marginalized through systems that keep them down speak up for themselves, God listens. This tells me that these women were not being divisive but enacting their own agency. God honored their standing up for what was right for themselves and the other women in their clan.

In August 2019 thousands of Indigenous women in Brazil declared "enough is enough" when they gathered to march and protest against right-wing president Jair Bolsonaro's plans to open up reservations to mining and agriculture, which could devastate the Amazon, the world's largest rain forest and home to hundreds of Indigenous people groups. Since Bolsonaro took office, there has been an upsurge in illegal invasions and deforestation. Throughout history, Indigenous people across the world have been fighting for their land rights, which were guaranteed by the United Nations Declaration on the Rights of Indigenous Peoples. It states that Indigenous groups have the right "not to be subjected to forced assimilation or destruction of their culture" or to be imperiled by "any action which has the aim or effect of dispossessing them of their lands, territories or resources."[8] The United Nations and the International Labour Organization's Indigenous and Tribal People's Convention also requires Indigenous consultation prior to engaging in anything that might exploit resources pertaining to their lands.

Bolsonaro's administration has not upheld these international agreements, prompting Indigenous women to step up and take the lead in protecting their lands and their rights. Joênia Wapichana was elected as the first Indigenous woman to ever serve in the Brazilian congress. Another Indigenous leader, Maria Eva Canoé, explains that Indigenous peoples "are resisting to exist,"[9] as many courageous and bold women throughout history have done and continue to do, women like Mahlah, Noah, Hoglah, Milcah, Tirzah—and women like Afro-Dominican farmer and activist Mamá Tingó.

Mamá Tingó was born November 8, 1921, in Villa Mella, Dominican Republic, to a family of poor farm workers. She and her husband, Felipe, made a living by working their farmland in Hato Viejo, Yamasá. In the early 1970s, an elite landowner named Pablo Díaz Hernández attempted to claim the land, aiming to displace Mamá Tingó and 350 families and campesinos, farmers, of Hato Viejo who had occupied the land for more than half a century.

Mamá Tingó became a leader in the Liga Agraria Cristiana, a Christian advocacy group for campesinos. She was baptized in the Parroquia Espíritu Santo, the Holy Spirit Church, in 1922, and her faith informed her activism for her community. She led the fight to ensure the rightful owners of the land could retain it. She did so through protests and marches, and like Mahlah, Noah, Hoglah, Milcah, and Tirzah, she even approached the president at the time. While he promised to distribute the land fairly, the president eventually broke his promise and sided with the rich business owner.

On November 1, 1974, Mamá Tingó led the farmers and the Liga Agraria Cristiana in a march demonstration. After marching up to Monte Plata court to have their case heard, several of the protestors—including Mamá Tingó—were arrested. Two days later, on the day of the hearing, Mamá Tingó was told that her pigs had been set loose. When she went to go gather them, she was shot and killed by Ernesto Diaz, one of Pablo Díaz Hernández's loyal followers. Some say the court hearing was a tactic used by Díaz Hernández to lure Mamá Tingó away from the land and momentarily let down her defenses.

Mamá Tingó was in her fifties when she led the fight, and as an older, uneducated, poor, Afro-Dominicana, she speaks to abuelita faith. She advocated and fought for herself and her community, giving her life as a martyr for the cause. We elevate and honor this often overlooked abuelita theologian.

⁂

While God vindicated Mahlah, Noah, Hoglah, Milcah, and Tirzah, it seems Moses didn't follow through. Joshua 17 shows that their God-given land was never granted to them. Many scholars, particularly womanists, have wondered if this is part of the reason why Moses wasn't allowed to enter the promised land.

The story doesn't end there, however.

In Joshua 17, we read that after Moses has died and Joshua takes his place, the sisters make yet another demand for their inheritance rights. This scenario plays out similarly to the last one: Mahlah, Noah, Hoglah, Milcah, and Tirzah approach the high priest, Eleazar, Joshua, and the leaders. They remind the men, "The LORD commanded Moses to give us a legacy along with our male relatives" (v. 4). Moses had failed to keep his end of the deal. Just like the first time, the women don't ask for their rights; they assert them, reminding the leaders that justice has still not been achieved and that they have not received what was promised by God.

The very next sentence reads that they were given a legacy along with their uncles.

Unlike Moses, Joshua grants them the land immediately—the tribal allotment is restated, and the inheritance of the women as daughters of Manasseh is repeated.[10]

Now, it's important to note the complicated space Mahlah, Noah, Hoglah, Milcah, and Tirzah inhabit. They are still caught within a patriarchal world, as is highlighted by their conversation with Moses in Numbers 36, where they agree to marry within their tribe. This means that the land given to them would be passed on to their future husbands. Reading these stories critically enables us to see how women resist, persist, and advocate for themselves, even if the patriarchy might prevail in the end. Their commitment to the struggle, la lucha, is a testament to women as we stand up for ourselves and one another in our fight for justice.

Their story is one of resolviendo, of doing what they can in the moment to ensure their survival. It is a story of bold mujeres who speak against injustice and inequity and of a God who listens and honors their cries.

———

Abuela ended up leaving the grocery store, but she didn't leave without a fight. In fact, with the help of my tía and tío (aunt and uncle), Abuela was able to keep a small portion of the cafeteria that was attached to it. To this day, Abuela still receives a little bit of money each month for rent of the cafeteria space.

For Abuela and many like her, resolviendo has always been and will always be a way of life. Many Latine scholars highlight this notion of daily survival as something that happens in lo cotidiano, the everyday. Lo cotidiano is central to resolviendo; it's the space where both God and structural and systemic sin are encountered most clearly.[11] It is where the oppressed live— socially marginalized, economically exploited, and struggling against sexism and ethnoracism.[12] Much theological discourse is dislodged from the actual lived experience of the majority of people, often turning lo cotidiano into an abstraction.

For example, the choices that a poor, single mother must make each day before nine in the morning are those that the majority of us don't have to think about—decisions that are intimately acquainted with survival. What will she do with the few dollars she has set aside for the day? How does this affect what she will eat or what she will feed her child? How does the weather, public transportation, her clothes, or lack thereof affect the decisions she'll have to make about sending her child to school or making it to work?

Lo cotidiano applies to embodied experiences, to practices and beliefs we have inherited—what we do with or how we deal with or face reality. Because it pertains to the marginalization of people in their daily lives, lo cotidiano is also the place where a new reality can be envisioned. When we begin to imagine a different world, a different societal structure, a different way of relating to the divine and ourselves, we can find creative and subversive ways to question and resist oppression.[13]

This is the space where God is most present, where God finds Godself in the details. It is the space where Jesus meets with the Samaritan woman and engages with her theologically as she is filling up her water jug. It is the space where Mary sits at Jesus's feet, learning from him as a disciple would. It is the space where Mahlah, Noah, Hoglah, Milcah, and Tirzah engage with God in order to receive rights that guarantee their survival.

It is also where Achsah, found in Joshua 15 and Judges 1, does similarly.

In Judges, Achsah is the first woman to be mentioned among a myriad of others—in fact, Judges identifies more individual women than any other book in the Hebrew Bible. She can be found alongside women like Deborah, the prophet and judge over Israel who leads the nation in battle, as well as Jael, who is famous for driving a tent peg through her opponent's temple, thus playing a part in leading the army to victory.

However, unlike Deborah and Jael, who receive a lot of praise for their bravery, Achsah's story isn't as celebrated or as frequently told. She is first introduced in Joshua 15:16 as Caleb's daughter, the same Caleb who was among the twelve that Moses sent to spy on Canaan. In the story, only Caleb and Joshua believed they could take it. Because of this, Caleb was promised descendants.

The main concern in both Joshua and Judges is the occupation of the land.[14] Like other books of the Bible, the book of Judges opens to a world of men's concerns, which besides land occupation included the concern of war. Leading up to Achsah's narrative, we learn about the continued efforts of the tribes of Israel to drive out the remaining people in Canaan in order to divide the land among the different tribes of Israel. The short story of Achsah is found amid a narrative of conquest that involves negotiating, maintaining, allotting, and defining boundaries.[15]

The first thing that we learn about Achsah in Judges is that she is caught as the object of one of these negotiations when her father seeks to trade her in a beneficial land acquisition to "the one who defeats and captures Kiriath-sepher" (Judg. 1:12)—a detail that reflects the patriarchal power of men over women. A man named Othniel turns out to be the victor, so Caleb follows through and delivers his daughter to him as a reward. Like the land around her, Achsah is shown to be a passive piece of property awarded to the military hero.[16] However, as the other women in these stories have shown us, land is livelihood—its dignity and ours are worth fighting for.

The story shifts when Othniel or Achsah decide to ask Caleb for more land. The Hebrew text is unclear who asks, so the question becomes, *Who prompts whom* to ask Caleb for the additional property (Josh. 15:18)? Many translations favor Achsah as the subject of the action, translating the Hebrew verb as "she urged him." However, other translators choose an alternate manuscript tradition, yielding "he urged her." The translator's role here is significant, as it alters the characterization of both Achsah and Othniel. This textual issue reflects a history of confusion about and interest in the gender dynamics of this story.[17]

While I agree with most translations that Achsah is the one who incites, urges, or convinces Othniel (instead of Othniel doing so to her), it's important to note the role of translation and interpretation. Someone once told me that they don't like the word *interpretation* because, to them, the Bible needs no interpretation; it just is what it is. Yet the textual issues in this passage are proof that such thinking can be dangerous. We have to remember that what we read has already been shaped by the biases, unintentional or not, of translators over centuries. As much as they may (or in some cases, may not) want to be objective, the process will always involve them not only choosing certain words over others but making decisions about where to put commas and periods and even what to capitalize. Oftentimes, we lack the words in English to appropriately translate ancient Hebrew or Greek. This should always be in the back of our minds when reading the Bible, urging us to read with an open mind, knowing that a lot goes into how we understand the text.

Nonetheless, Achsah is the one who prompts the asking for more land, demonstrating that she understands what is important in her world. Some argue that she is being manipulative. While manipulation often has a negative connotation, it is a common tactic for women in oppressive situations. Perhaps Achsah, like many other women in Scripture, took advantage of the system for her own survival.

Whether Achsah is using manipulation or not, her actions stand in stark contrast to her image as a passive piece of property, a prize woman. Instead, she becomes a smart and determined woman, one who knows how to operate within the constraints of her society. And as Jewish scholar Lillian Klein points out, her active position does not make her husband passive any more than her intelligence makes him stupid.[18] Perhaps the intelligence of her husband, Othniel, is shown through his willingness to listen to his wife's suggestion since she might have insider information concerning her father's circumstance. After all, Proverbs 31 praises women who use their wisdom to benefit their families.

In the very next sentence, we find Achsah talking to her father. Putting all previous textual issues aside, we'd still notice that Achsah is the one who gets on her donkey and travels (alone, according to the text) to see her father. Caleb asks his daughter, "What do you want?" (Josh. 15:18). At this point, what she wants from him is twofold. Her surprising assertiveness is evident from her first words to her father, expressed in the Hebrew imperative verb form: "Give me a blessing [or present]" (15:19). Achsah alone crafts the language of the request. And the outcome?

Caleb gives his daughter the upper and lower springs (15:19).

In the end, Achsah is the one who, despite her circumstances, successfully accomplishes the goal of acquiring more land, her shrewd words possibly connecting the unfavorable land she has been given to her own diminished value in her patriarchal world (15:19).

This narrative is, once again, an example of the interstitial space marginalized women in a patriarchal world inhabit. While Achsah is traded as a piece of property, subject to her culture, she does not remain silent or passive. Achsah shows that she is a woman who knows how to live within the constraints of her society. She recognizes what is important for her in that social milieu, and her working within the system proves her wisdom. She is also a woman who acts decisively, adjusting her method to the situation at hand. Achsah acquires more land from her father and gives voice to her condition in a way that is unusual and noteworthy in the patriarchal world of the Bible, in a way akin to that of Mahlah, Noah, Hoglah, Milcah, and Tirzah.[19]

Many poor and marginalized women of color in the US have experienced situations similar to that of Abuela's. "Latinxs in general and Latinas in particular are perennial outsiders, treated as non-bodies within racist, classist and sexist structures that permeate US society."[20] Many women of color in the US live in neighborhoods where they must struggle daily for basic necessities like fresh and sanitary food; safe living conditions, including heat and water; quality education for their children; and other aspects of a decent quality of life. Growing up, Mom remembers rat-infested homes, Peeping Toms, and other things that she spent her adult life working to shield me from. "Life is a perennial struggle. They struggle not just for themselves, but also for their families and communities."[21]

After Papi died, Abuela's priority became keeping her part of the store. It was her vocation, what ensured her survival. In his book *Nobody Cries When We Die*, Patrick Reyes talks about how in many Christian conversations we think vocation is "God calling us out of our present reality and into some divinely purposed and infinitely better future. Unfortunately, life does not always allow this to occur. In fact, God often just calls us to survive."[22] This is true for most people in the world; their Christian calling is simply survival.

When we talk about vocation in privileged spaces, we forget that surviving, resolviendo, is holy too—a sacred endeavor.

Ada Maria Isasi-Díaz says that "la vida es la lucha—the struggle is life." She explains that for over half of her life, she thought her task was to struggle and then one day enjoy the fruits of her labor—"but above all I have realized that I can and should relish the struggle," she says. "The struggle is my life; my dedication to the struggle is one of the main driving forces in my life." Relishing the struggle involves recognizing God's presence within it, realizing that the struggle is sacred. And while la lucha is a personal struggle for survival, it also marks our collective struggle for liberation.[23]

This is central to the stories of Achsah, Noah, Hoglah, Milcah, Tirzah, the Indigenous women of Brazil, and Mamá Tingó—as their fights centered on the land and their need to resolver in connection to it. They struggled not only for themselves but for the generations of women after them. As Aboriginal elder Lilla Watson articulates so beautifully, our liberation is bound together.[24] And that too—our collective struggle—is holy.

I think Paul speaks to this. In Romans 8:18–25 he reminds us that as we cry out to be set free, so does creation. I wonder where Paul got this idea. Did he learn it from his ancestors: how interconnected and beautifully intertwined we all are with all created things? I often think that the creation itself understands la lucha of survival—as it groans and protests, so do we.

Similarly, in his book *The Christian Imagination*, Willie Jennings argues that we cannot talk about the struggle of body and soul without talking about earth and land. Since the beginning of creation, human beings have been commissioned to watch over the earth, take care of it, and receive nourishment from it. The connection among God's creation—land, animals, and humans—in the narrative is beautiful, divine, "very good." This human connection to the land and to animals isn't just something we see in the creation narrative; it continues to play out across time and across communities.[25] This is why much of Israel's story is deeply rooted in land—their displacement from it and their longing to be restored in it.

Throughout history, coming across a people also meant coming across the land they were connected to and the animals that were a part of their family. It's a divine sense of "creaturely entanglement," Jennings explains.[26] We've always lived in an enmeshed world where our lives are intertwined and continuously interweaving. This is why the effects of colonization and land displacement are so detrimental. What was once a holistic identity, one that mirrored the goodness of creation, now becomes a distorted identity. Because of this, resistance and decolonizing work must involve restoring these broken and distorted identities.

This is why I often find myself going back to moments with Abuela when we both reconnected with the land, the earth.

Some of my most powerful memories include digging, planting, and learning how to tend the dirt with Abuela. I'd spend hours with her outside, picking the best mangoes from the trees for our afternoon snack while listening to her stories of life on the island. Abuela always reminded me that Cuba es la isla más bella del mundo (Cuba is the most beautiful island in the world). She loved her garden, and that is the place where I saw her come to life, where she found restoration and wholeness. Jennings explains that bodies are at home in the dirt. Black and Brown bodies that have been subjugated, displaced, or seen as foreign, and their movements that are seen as inappropriate, find their home among the trees and the animals.[27]

I was raised by Abuela's mango and avocado trees. They hold secrets and stories from my childhood. I was also raised by the mamoncillos—the ones we purchased every week from the man at the intersection of Flagler Street and 97th Avenue for a couple dollars. Mom and I would rip the small bag open, break through the skin of the fruit, and suck its sour goodness. It gave us of itself. Like the trees in Abuela's yard, the mamoncillos, too, hold stories: stories of resolviendo, of survival and exile and nights spent walking up and down Calle Ocho selling fruit in order to make enough to feed the family that night.

We always brought home a bag for Abuela too, because the earth's gifts are meant to be shared.

Abuela still lives in the duplex where I was raised, where the majority of her years en la lucha were spent. The same wallpaper still sticks to the walls; the same picture frames—some updated—still rest on her glass coffee table. The same little shed sits in the middle of her yard. Abuela doesn't get out of bed much these days. Her body is too fragile. When I talk to her on the phone, our conversations often consist of one constant loop, "¿Ya comiste? ¿Te sientes bien?" (Have you eaten? Do you feel good?) Loving someone with dementia has felt like a lot of little deaths.

While living in Los Angeles, I'd fly home regularly to visit her. During my earlier visits, she loved to spend time among her plants and her trees in the backyard—before her legs started giving out. On one particularly warm Miami day, she wanted to check on the mangoes across the yard, so she grabbed my arm and we slowly made our way, one small step at a time.

"¿Sabes que Cuba es la isla más bella del mundo?" (Did you know Cuba is the most beautiful island in the world?)

"Sí, yo lo sé." (Yes, I know.)

As we walked hand in hand, her face lit up as she recalled memories of the grocery store in Little Havana during those early years, which she often confuses with her time in Cuba. In her mind, they run together. A detail I don't wish to correct.

When we arrived at her mango tree, she rested her body against it and asked me to grab for her the wooden broom in the kitchen that she has had for decades, so she could attempt to knock a fruit off. We laughed as I held her tight while she swung and swung, barely getting close to hitting a branch. One finally fell and we grabbed it off the ground. She held it and inspected it, squeezed it between her frail fingers.

I realize now the weight of that small fruit in her hands. It tells a story of sustenance, of survival, of resolviendo. It tells a story of la lucha.

"Vamos a comer" (Let's eat), she said.

Before we made our slow trek back to the house, I asked her to stop against the chain-link fence.

"Quiero tirarte una foto" (I want to take a picture of you), I told her.

I'm so glad I captured that moment. Her smile, her mango in hand. I just knew she was in her element.

For it is at the site of the dirt that we are joined. And the dirt is our kin. From dust we came, and to dust we will return. We are creatures of the dirt, bound together.[28]

Notes

Chapter 1 Research Grief

1. The term *Latine* is used in place of *Latino/a* as a way to highlight the diversity of the Latino/a experience in gender, sexuality, nationality, place of birth, etc. I use *Latine* when referring to the Latino/a community in a general or more academic sense. I use *Latina* when referring to my own personal experiences.

2. Serano, *Excluded*, 44. See also Collins, *Black Feminist Thought*.

3. *Abuela* is the formal term for grandmother while *abuelita* is more like a term of endearment, similar to *granny* in English.

4. De La Torre, *Quest for the Cuban Christ*, 3.

5. De La Torre, *Quest for the Cuban Christ*, 3.

6. M. Gonzalez, *Afro-Cuban Theology*, 22.

7. Anzaldúa, *Light in the Dark/Luz en lo oscuro*, "Preface: Gestures of the Body."

8. De La Torre, *Quest for the Cuban Christ*, 3.

9. De La Torre, *Quest for the Cuban Christ*, 5.

10. Guardiola-Sáenz, "Border-Crossing and Its Redemptive Power," 129.

11. Donaldson, "Sign of Orpah," 95.

12. Menchú and Burgos-Debray, *I, Rigoberta Menchú*. See chap. 18, "The Bible and Self-defence: The Examples of Judith, Moses and David."

13. M. Gonzalez, *Afro-Cuban Theology*, 75.

14. De La Torre, *La Lucha for Cuba*, 30.

15. Pedraza, "Los Marielitos of 1980."

16. De La Torre, *La Lucha for Cuba*, 15.

17. De La Torre, *La Lucha for Cuba*, 25.

18. De La Torre, *La Lucha for Cuba*, 32.

Chapter 2 Abuelita Theology

1. *Interstitial* is a word that means forming or occupying interstices, which are small spaces like cracks or crevices.

2. Rodríguez and Fortier, *Cultural Memory*, 1–4.

3. Hasan Al-Saidi, "Post-colonialism Literature," 95–105.

4. Hasan Al-Saidi, "Post-colonialism Literature," 95.

5. Hasan Al-Saidi, "Post-colonialism Literature," 96.

6. "John MacArthur Beth Moore Go Home."

7. Armas, "White Peacemakers," 16:48–17:08 mins.

8. M. Smith, *I Found God in Me*, 8.

9. Isasi-Díaz, *Mujerista Theology*, 1.

10. Isasi-Díaz, *Mujerista Theology*, 3.

11. Isasi-Díaz, *Mujerista Theology*, 1.

12. Isasi-Díaz, *Mujerista Theology*, 2–3.

13. Aquino and Nuñez, *Feminist Intercultural Theology*, xv–xxv.

14. In Spanish, the Holy Spirit is typically referred to in masculine terms (el Espíritu Santo); however, in an attempt to mirror the feminine references to the Holy Spirit in Scripture, I often use the feminine term: la Espíritu Santa.

15. Martell-Otero, Maldonado Pérez, and Conde-Frazier, *Latina Evangélicas*, 14.

16. Romero, "Spiritual Praxis of Cesar Chavez," 24–39.

17. Garcia, *Gospel of César Chávez*, 26–27.

18. Romero, "Spiritual Praxis of Cesar Chavez," 27–28.

19. Romero, "Spiritual Praxis of Cesar Chavez," 24.

20. Jennings, *After Whiteness*, 6.

21. Jennings, *After Whitness*, 7.

22. Santos, *Epistemologies of the South*, 42.

23. Tippett, "Robin Wall Kimmerer," 22:00.

24. Tippett, "Robin Wall Kimmerer," 36:00.

25. Lee, *We Will Get to the Promised Land*, 51.

26. Lee, *We Will Get to the Promised Land*, 52.

27. Thurman, *Jesus and the Disinherited*, chap. 2.

28. Byers, "Native American Grandmothers," 305–16.

29. Mutchler, Baker, and Lee, "Grandparents Responsible for Grandchildren," 990–1009.

30. Tinker, *Spirit and Resistance*, loc. 1472–2066.

31. Yoshinori, "Asian Grandparents."

32. Keegan and Carlson, *Talking Taíno*, 5.

33. Martell-Otero, Maldonado Pérez, and Conde-Frazier, *Latinas Evangélicas*, 3.

34. Martell-Otero, Maldonado Pérez, and Conde-Frazier, *Latinas Evangélicas*, 2.

35. Zaru, "Biblical Teachings," 89.

36. Balthasar, *Credo*, 85.

Chapter 3 A Sabiduría That Heals

1. Anzaldúa and Keating, *This Bridge We Call Home*, 541–42.
2. Brownsworth, *Lost to the West*, 14.
3. Medina and Gonzales, *Voices from the Ancestors*, 8.
4. Medina and Gonzales, *Voices from the Ancestors*, 11.
5. See the Young Living Essential Oils blog: "Essential Oils in the Ancient World: Part II." See also Gemi-Iordanou et al., *Medicine, Healing and Performance*.
6. Abelsoud, "Herbal Medicine in Ancient Egypt." See also Gemi-Iordanou et al., *Medicine, Healing and Performance*, 34.
7. I'd like to add that I'm not against Western medicine. I am thankful for modern science, as it is essential for many forms of healing and managing pain, depression, anxiety, etc. I'm not arguing that Indigenous forms of healing should replace Western medicine; I'm just questioning why it's historically been demonized, in a spiritual sense, particularly by Christians who are now embracing those same practices.
8. Carolina Hinojosa-Cisneros, Facebook, August 18, 2020.
9. Rivera, "God at the Crossroads," 240.
10. Rivera, "God at the Crossroads," 242.
11. Rivera, "God at the Crossroads," 242–43.
12. Martell-Otero, Maldonado Pérez, and Conde-Frazier, *Latinas Evangélicas*, 14.
13. G. Smith, *Historical Geography*, 244; Bright, *History of Israel*, 360.
14. Hamori, *Women's Divination*, 138.
15. Bellis, *Helpmates, Harlots, and Heroes*, 155.
16. Camp, "Wise Women of 2 Samuel," 14–29.
17. Camp, "Wise Women of 2 Samuel," 14–29.
18. Romero, *Brown Church*, 90.
19. Romero, *Brown Church*, 92.
20. Romero, *Brown Church*, 93.
21. Romero, *Brown Church*, 96–97.
22. Pinto-Bailey and dos Reis, "'Slave Woman,'" 207.

Chapter 4 Mujeres of Exodus

1. Curtice, *Native*, 17.
2. Warrior, "Canaanites, Cowboys, and Indians," 21–26.
3. Zaru, "Biblical Teachings," 86.
4. Warrior, "Canaanites, Cowboys, and Indians," 25.
5. Gafney, "When Gomer Looks More like God."
6. Gutiérrez, *We Drink from Our Own Wells*, 77.
7. Chase, *Revolution within the Revolution*, 22.
8. Chase, *Revolution within the Revolution*, 22.
9. Chase, *Revolution within the Revolution*, 28.
10. Robinson, *Montgomery Bus Boycott*, 15.

11. Robinson, *Montgomery Bus Boycott*, 8.
12. Meyers, *Households and Holiness*, 34.
13. Berlyn, "Pharaohs Who Knew Moses," 5.
14. Lapsley, *Whispering the Word*, 72.
15. Lapsley, *Whispering the Word*, 73.
16. Meyers, *Households and Holiness*, 39.
17. Gafney, *Womanist Midrash*, 91.
18. Frymer-Kensky, "Saviors of the Exodus," 25–26.
19. Gafney, *Womanist Midrash*, 90.
20. Jones, "Oldest Trick in the Book," 163–64.
21. Weems, "Hebrew Women Are Not Like the Egyptian Women," 29.
22. Frymer-Kensky, "Saviors of the Exodus," 26.
23. Gafney, *Womanist Midrash*, 91.
24. Evans, *Searching for Sunday*, 3.
25. Nikondeha, *Defiant*, 206–7.
26. Lapsley, *Whispering the Word*, 74.
27. Martell-Otero, Maldonado Pérez, and Conde-Frazier, *Latinas Evangélicas*, 41–42.

Chapter 5 Telling La Verdad

1. In recent years, some have pointed out the dangers of this show, how it sexually objectified women and girls. See Jaramillo, "Queasy Cultural Legacy."
2. "Mother Teresa Reflects."
3. Lewis, "35 Zora Neale Hurston Quotes."
4. In the Hebrew Bible, Nazirites were Israelites who made vows to consecrate themselves to the service of God.
5. Meyers, "Hannah and Her Sacrifice," 97.
6. Stringer, "Hannah," 3.
7. Meyers, "Hannah Narrative in Feminist Perspective," 117.
8. Meyers, "Hannah and Her Sacrifice," 94.
9. Klein, "Hannah," 89.
10. Klein, "Hannah," 88.
11. Amit, "Am I Not More," 75.
12. Klein, "Hannah," 90–91.
13. Stringer, "Hannah," 4.
14. Rachel Held Evans, Twitter, October 27, 2016, https://twitter.com/rachelheldevans/status/791747847251189761.
15. Klein, "Hannah," 90.
16. Klein, "Hannah," 86.
17. Klein, "Hannah," 92.
18. Martell-Otero, Maldonado Pérez, and Conde-Frazier, *Latinas Evangélicas*, 88.
19. M. Smith, *I Found God in Me*, 2.
20. Anzaldúa, *Anzaldúa Reader*, 48.
21. Loera-Brus, "Latinos Owe African Americans."

Chapter 6 Cosiendo and Creating

1. Carolina Hinojosa-Cisneros, Facebook, December 20, 2020.
2. Gibbs, *Household Textiles*, 1.
3. Siegal, *Aymara-Bolivianische Textilien*, 15–16.
4. For example, young women in traditional Malian culture wear *bogolan* tunics around their wastes as spiritual protection during the liminal periods following their initiations into womanhood, marriage, and childbirth. See Allman, *Fashioning Africa*, 194.
5. Medina and Gonzales, *Voices from the Ancestors*, 73.
6. See "Rana Plaza Accident."
7. See Moulds, "Child Labour."
8. Mehta, "Beyond Recycling."
9. See "Chilean President Salvador Allende."
10. See Barros, *Constitutionalism and Dictatorship*.
11. Agosín, "Arpilleras of Chile."
12. Inés Velásquez-McBryde, conversation with the author, August 16, 2020.
13. Inés Velásquez-McBryde, conversation with the author, August 16, 2020.
14. Witherington, "Joanna," 12–14.
15. Medina and Gonzales, *Voices from the Ancestors*, 73.
16. Medina and Gonzalez, *Voices from the Ancestors*, 78.
17. Dickerson, "Acts 9:36–43," 301.
18. Aymer, "Acts of the Apostles," 541–42.
19. Keener, *Acts*, 2:1716.
20. Dickerson, "Acts 9:36–43," 302.
21. Kohles, "Euodia, Syntyche, and Lydia," 44.
22. Kohles, "Euodia, Syntyche, and Lydia," 44.
23. Esther Díaz Martín, "Aprender bordando: Embroidery as Meditation and Knowledge Making," in Medina and Gonzales, *Voices from the Ancestors*, 80.

Chapter 7 Sobreviviendo

1. K. González, *God Who Sees*, 31.
2. Honig, "Ruth, the Model Emigrée," 52.
3. Norton, "Silenced Struggles for Survival," 267.
4. Meyers, "Returning Home," 91, 109–10.
5. Donaldson, "Sign of Orpah," 101.
6. Donaldson, "Sign of Orpah," 101.
7. Meyers, "Family in Early Israel," 21–22.
8. Stevenson, *Just Mercy*, 12–14.
9. Norton, "Silenced Struggles for Survival," 266–67.
10. Norton, "Silenced Struggles for Survival," 269.
11. Armas, "Cultural Identity, Liminality & Folklore."
12. Norton, "Silenced Struggles for Survival," 270.
13. Chan, "Ultimate Trickster," 93.

14. Trible, "Human Comedy," 161.
15. De La Torre, *Embracing Hopelessness*, 150.
16. De La Torre, *Embracing Hopelessness*, 151.
17. Jackson, *Comedy and Feminist Interpretation*, 41.
18. Chan, "Ultimate Trickster," 94–97.
19. Chan, "Ultimate Trickster," 98.
20. Chan, "Ultimate Trickster," 96.
21. Fuchs, "Status and Role," 77.
22. Fuchs, "Status and Role," 80.
23. Fuchs, "Status and Role," 48.

Chapter 8 Protesta and Persistence

1. Drabold, "Meet the Mothers."
2. Morrison, "Here's Everything You Need to Know."
3. For image, see Spalding, "When George Floyd Called Out."
4. Branch, *Jeroboam's Wife*, 34–35.
5. Gafney, *Womanist Midrash*, 198.
6. M. Fernandez, "'You Have to Pay With Your Body.'"
7. According to a 2016 National Institute of Justice study. See *Missing and Murdered*.
8. Branch, *Jeroboam's Wife*, 35.
9. Gafney, *Womanist Midrash*, 199.
10. Gafney, *Womanist Midrash*, 199
11. Evans, *Inspired*, 111.
12. Peterson, *Word Made Flesh*, chap. 3.
13. Sacks, *Haggadah*, 106.
14. Gafney, *Womanist Midrash*, 200.
15. Deut. 21:23 states that bodies were to be buried the same day and not left on the ground as to pollute it.
16. Branch, *Jeroboam's Wife*, 35.
17. Gafney, *Womanist Midrash*, 201.
18. Branch, *Jeroboam's Wife*, 52.
19. McSherry, "Operation Condor."
20. Renée Epelbaum in Muñoz and Portillo, *Mothers of Plaza De Mayo*, 20:48 min.
21. Renée Epelbaum in Muñoz and Portillo, *Mothers of Plaza De Mayo*, 25:05 min.
22. Renée Epelbaum in Muñoz and Portillo, *Mothers of Plaza De Mayo*, 23:09 min.
23. Hebe de Bonafini in Muñoz and Portillo, *Mothers of Plaza De Mayo*, 36:36 min.
24. Bellucci, "Childless Motherhood," 87
25. Bellucci, "Childless Motherhood," 83–88.
26. "Cuba's 'Ladies in White.'"
27. Reid, "A Godly Widow," 28.

Chapter 9 Desesperación

1. For ethnic/racial bias see Hall et al., "Implicit Racial/Ethnic Bias." For gender bias, see Samulowitz et al., "'Brave Men' and 'Emotional Women.'"
2. For more information, see Penner et al., "Reducing Racial Health Care Disparities."
3. Fiorenza, *But She Said*, 13.
4. Martell-Otero, Maldonado Pérez, and Conde-Frazier, *Latinas Evangélicas*, 86.
5. Saldaña, "Orale!," 1.
6. Lopez and Robles, "Latina Evangélicas Panel Discussion," 9:54–11:15 mins.
7. Martell-Otero, Maldonado Pérez, and Conde-Frazier, *Latinas Evangélicas*, 3.
8. Kohn, Quiñones, and Robinson, *Hermanas*, 56.
9. A citizen of Botswana.
10. Dube, *Postcolonial Feminist Interpretation*, 145.
11. Fiorenza, *But She Said*, 14.
12. Dube, *Postcolonial Feminist Interpretation*, 147.
13. Keener, *Commentary on the Gospel of Matthew*, 263.
14. Osborne and Arnold, *Matthew*, 597.
15. Love, *Jesus and Marginal Women*, 159.
16. Kam, *Their Stories, Our Stories*, 194–97.
17. Levine and Brettler, *Jewish Annotated New Testament*, 3.
18. Love, *Jesus and Marginal Women*, 162.
19. Dube, *Postcolonial Feminist Interpretation*, 149.
20. Dube, *Postcolonial Feminist Interpretation*, 139.
21. Fiorenza, *But She Said*, 14.
22. Dube, *Postcolonial Feminist Interpretation*, 193.
23. Fiorenza, *But She Said*, 11.
24. Fiorenza, *But She Said*, 12.
25. Limón, "Wonder Woman."
26. Leahy, "What Does It Mean."

Chapter 10 A Divine Baile

1. S. Fernández, "Celia Cruz's 'Son Con Guaguancó.'"
2. Figueroa, "Toward a Spiritual Pedagogy," 40.
3. Leseho and Maxell, "Coming Alive," 17.
4. Martell-Otero, Maldonado Pérez, and Conde-Frazier, *Latinas Evangélicas*, 41.
5. Martell-Otero, Maldonado Pérez, and Conde-Frazier, *Latinas Evangélicas*, 40
6. Kramer, "Miriam," 109.
7. Kramer, "Miriam," 109.
8. Crosley, "Nipple and the Damage Done."
9. Kreps, "Nipple Ripples."
10. Markham, *Journal of Christopher Columbus*, 38.

11. Zinn, *People's History*, chap. 1.
12. Fallas, "In the Garden of Eden."
13. Conde-Fraizer, "Hispanic Protestant Spirituality," 139.
14. O'Day, "Gospel of John," 630.
15. Guardiola-Sáenz, "Border-Crossing and Its Redemptive Power," 142.
16. Althaus-Reid, *Queer God*, 2.
17. Althaus-Reid, *Queer God*, 2.
18. Martell-Otero, Maldonado Pérez, and Conde-Frazier, *Latinas Evangélicas*, 14. Bachata is a Caribbean style of dance in which you dance with a partner.
19. Ramsey, *This Too Shall Last*, 37.
20. Van der Kolk, *Body Keeps the Score*, 102.
21. Elizondo, *Future Is Mestizo*, xiv.
22. Darden, *Scripturalizing Revelation*, 64.
23. Darden, *Scripturalizing Revelation*, 64.
24. Anzaldúa, *Anzaldúa Reader*, 49.
25. Anzaldúa, *Anzaldúa Reader*, 9.

Chapter 11 Madre of Exile

1. J. González, *Mañana*, 41.
2. De La Torre, *La Lucha for Cuba*, 22.
3. García-Johnson, *Spirit Outside the Gate*, 116.
4. "Walter Mignolo 'Colonial Wounds.'"
5. García-Johnson, *Spirit Outside the Gate*, 131.
6. M. Gonzalez, *Afro-Cuban Theology*, 82–83.
7. Tweed, *Our Lady of the Exile*, 23.
8. Tweed, *Our Lady of the Exile*, 29.
9. García-Rivera, *Community of the Beautiful*, 5.
10. Hidalgo, *Revelation in Aztlán*, 18.
11. Altahus-Reid, *Indecent Theology*, 66.
12. Althaus-Reid, *Indecent Theology*, 75.
13. Althaus-Reid, *Indecent Theology*, 34.
14. Althaus-Reid, *Indecent Theology*, 59.
15. Althaus-Reid, *Indecent Theology*, 44.
16. Ruether, *Sexism and God-Talk*, 153.
17. McCaulley, *Reading While Black*, 85.
18. McCaulley, *Reading While Black*, 86.
19. Ruether, *Sexism and God-Talk*, 156–57.
20. Anzaldúa, *Anzaldúa Reader*, 243.

Chapter 12 Resolviendo in La Lucha

1. García-Alfonso, *Resolviendo*, 106.
2. García-Alfonso, *Resolviendo*, 106.
3. García-Alfonso, *Resolviendo*, 107.
4. Gafney, *Womanist Midrash*, 159.

5. Gafney, *Womanist Midrash*, 144.

6. Gafney, *Womanist Midrash*, 144.

7. Gafney, *Womanist Midrash*, 144.

8. UN General Assembly, Resolution 61/295, art. 8, nos. 1 and 2b.

9. Mendes, "Resisting to Exist."

10. Gafney, *Womanist Midrash*, 148.

11. Martell-Otero, Maldonado Pérez, and Conde-Frazier, *Latinas Evangélicas*, 41.

12. Isasi-Díaz, "Mujerista Discourse," 49.

13. Isasi-Díaz, "Mujerista Discourse," 49.

14. Klein, "Achsah," 19.

15. Newsom, Ringe, and Lapsley, *Women's Bible Commentary*.

16. Newsom, Ringe, and Lapsley, *Women's Bible Commentary*, 107.

17. Newsom, Ringe, and Lapsley, *Women's Bible Commentary*, 107.

18. Klein, "Achsah," 24.

19. Newsom, Ringe, and Lapsley, *Women's Bible Commentary*, 107.

20. Martell-Otero, Maldonado Pérez, and Conde-Frazier, *Latinas Evangélicas*, 36.

21. Martell-Otero, Maldonado Pérez, and Conde-Frazier, *Latinas Evangélicas*, 36.

22. Reyes, *Nobody Cries When We Die*.

23. All quotes in this paragraph are from Isasi-Díaz, *Mujerista Theology*, chap. 1, "A Hispanic Garden in a Foreign Land," 13–28.

24. Watson was heard delivering this quote at the 1985 United Nations Decade for Women Conference in Nairobi. However, she has explained that in the early 1970s she was part of an aboriginal rights group in Queensland, where together they came up with the phrase.

25. See Jennings, *Christian Imagination*.

26. Labberton, "Willie James Jennings on Race."

27. Labberton, "Willie James Jennings on Race."

28. Jennings, "Can 'White' People Be Saved."

Bibliography

Abelsoud, N. H. "Herbal Medicine in Ancient Egypt." *Journal of Medicinal Plants Research* 4, no. 2 (January 18, 2010): 82–86.

Agosín, Marjorie. "The Arpilleras of Chile (with Marjorie Agosin)." Video. Facing History and Ourselves. Accessed July 17, 2020. https://www.facing history.org/resource-library/video/arpilleras-chile-marjorie-agosin.

Allman, Jean Marie. *Fashioning Africa: Power and the Politics of Dress.* African Expressive Cultures. Bloomington: Indiana University Press, 2004.

Althaus-Reid, Marcella. *Indecent Theology: Theological Perversions in Sex, Gender and Politics.* New York: Routledge, 2000.

———. *The Queer God.* London: Routledge, 2003.

Amit, Yairah. "Am I Not More Devoted to You than Ten Sons? (1 Samuel 1.8): Male and Female Interpretations." In Brenner, *Samuel and Kings,* 68–76.

Anzaldúa, Gloria. *The Gloria Anzaldúa Reader.* Edited by AnaLouise Keating. Durham, NC: Duke University Press, 2009.

———. *Light in the Dark/Luz en lo oscuro: Rewriting Identity, Spirituality, Reality.* Edited by AnaLouise Keating. Durham, NC: Duke University Press, 2015.

Anzaldúa, Gloria, and AnaLouise Keating, eds. *This Bridge We Call Home: Radical Visions of Transformation.* New York: Routledge, 2002.

Aquino, María Pilar, and María José Rosado Nuñez, eds. *Feminist Intercultural Theology: Latina Explorations for a Just World*. Maryknoll, NY: Orbis Books, 2007.

Armas, Kat. "Anti-racism as Spiritual Formation (Ally Henny Pt. 2)." Posted September 30, 2020. *The Protagonistas*. Podcast, 56:27. https://katarmas .com/theprotagonistaspodcast/2020/9/30/anti-racism-as-spiritual-for mation-ally-henny-pt-2.

———. "Cultural Identity, Liminality & Folklore." Posted July 31, 2020. *The Protagonistas*. Podcast, 51:36. https://katarmas.com/theprotagonis taspodcast/2020/7/31/cultural-identity-liminality-amp-folklore.

———. "White Peacemakers and Holistic, Sustainable Restoration." Posted May 26, 2020. *The Protagonistas*. Podcast, 43:30. https://katarmas.com /theprotagonistaspodcast/2020/5/26/white-peacemakers-and-holistic -sustainable-restoration.

Aymer, Margaret. "Acts of the Apostles." In Newsom, Ringe, and Lapsley, *Women's Bible Commentary*, 536–46. Louisville: Westminster John Knox, 2012.

Bach, Alice, ed. *Women in the Hebrew Bible: A Reader*. Hoboken, NJ: Taylor and Francis, 2013.

Balthasar, Hans Urs von. *Credo: Meditations on the Apostle's Creed*. Twentieth Century Religious Thought. San Francisco: Ignatius, 2005.

Barros, Robert. *Constitutionalism and Dictatorship: Pinochet, the Junta, and the 1980 Constitution*. Cambridge Studies in the Theory of Democracy. Cambridge: Cambridge University Press, 2002.

Bellis, Alice Ogden. *Helpmates, Harlots, and Heroes: Women's Stories in the Hebrew Bible*. Louisville: Westminster John Knox, 1994.

Bellucci, Mabel. "Childless Motherhood: Interview with Nora Cortiñas, a Mother of the Plaza de Mayo, Argentina." *Reproductive Health Matters* 7, no. 13 (1999): 83–88.

Berlyn, Patricia. "The Pharaohs Who Knew Moses." *Jewish Bible Quarterly* 39, no. 1 (January 2011): 3–14.

Branch, Robin. *Jeroboam's Wife: The Enduring Contributions of the Old Testament's Least-Known Women*. Grand Rapids: Baker Academic, 2009.

Brenner, Athalya, ed. *Exodus to Deuteronomy*. A Feminist Companion to the Bible. Sheffield: Sheffield Academic, 2000.

———. *Judges*. A Feminist Companion to the Bible. Sheffield: JSOT Press, 1993.

———. *Ruth and Esther*. A Feminist Companion to the Bible. Eugene, OR: Wipf & Stock, 2007.

———. *Samuel and Kings*. A Feminist Companion to the Bible. Sheffield: Sheffield Academic, 1994.

Bright, J. *A History of Israel*. 4th ed. Louisville: Westminster John Knox, 1959.

Brownworth, Lars. *Lost to the West: The Forgotten Byzantine Empire That Rescued Western Civilization*. New York: Crown, 2010.

Byers, L. "Native American Grandmothers: Cultural Tradition and Contemporary Necessity." *Journal of Ethnic & Cultural Diversity in Social Work* 19, no. 4 (2010): 305–16.

Camp, Claudia V. "The Wise Women of 2 Samuel: A Role Model for Women in Early Israel." *Catholic Biblical Quarterly* 43 (1981): 14–29.

Chan, C. W. "The Ultimate Trickster in the Story of Tamar from a Feminist Perspective." *Feminist Theology* 24, no. 1 (2015): 93–101.

Chase, Michelle. *Revolution within the Revolution: Women and Gender Politics in Cuba, 1952–1962*. Envisioning Cuba. Chapel Hill: University of North Carolina Press, 2015.

"Chilean President Salvador Allende Dies in Coup." History.com, September 9, 2020. https://www.history.com/this-day-in-history/allende-dies-in-coup.

Collins, Patricia Hill. *Black Feminist Thought: Knowledge, Consciousness, and the Politics of Empowerment*. New York: Routledge, 2000.

Conde-Frazier, Elizabeth. "Hispanic Protestant Spirituality." In *Teología en Conjunto: A Collaborative Hispanic Protestant Theology*, edited by José David Rodriguez and Loida I. Martell-Otero, 125–45. Louisville: Westminster John Knox, 1997.

Crosley, Hillary. "The Nipple and the Damage Done: Janet Jackson's Post-Super Bowl Fall." Music, *Rolling Stone*, January 31, 2014. https://www.rollingstone.com/music/music-news/the-nipple-and-the-damage-done-janet-jacksons-post-super-bowl-fall-187061/.

"Cuba's 'Ladies in White.'" Human Rights *First*. Accessed January 12, 2021. https://web.archive.org/web/20090720010456/http://www.humanrightsfirst.org/defenders/hrd_cuba/hrd_cuba_blanco.htm.

Curtice, Kaitlin B. *Native: Identity, Belonging, and Rediscovering God*. Grand Rapids: Brazos, 2020.

Darden, Lynne St. Clair. *Scripturalizing Revelation: An African American Postcolonial Reading of Empire.* Atlanta: SBL Press, 2015.

De La Torre, Miguel A. *Embracing Hopelessness.* Minneapolis: Fortress, 2017.

————. *Hispanic American Religious Cultures.* Santa Barbara, CA: ABC-CLIO, 2009.

————. *La Lucha for Cuba: Religion and Politics on the Streets of Miami.* Berkeley: University of California Press, 2003.

————. *The Quest for the Cuban Christ: A Historical Search.* The History of African-American Religions. Gainesville: University Press of Florida, 2002.

Dickerson, Febbie C. "Acts 9:36–43: The Many Faces of Tabitha, a Womanist Reading." In M. Smith, *I Found God in Me,* 296–312.

Donaldson, Laura. "The Sign of Orpah: Reading Ruth through Native Eyes." In Kwok, *Hope Abundant,* 138–51.

Drabold, Will. "Meet the Mothers of the Movement Speaking at the Democratic Convention." Politics, *Time,* July 26, 2015. https://time.com/4423920/dnc-mothers-movement-speakers/.

Dube, Musa. *Postcolonial Feminist Interpretation of the Bible.* St. Louis: Chalice, 2014.

Elizondo, Virgilio P. *The Future Is Mestizo: Life Where Cultures Meet.* Rev. ed. Boulder: University Press of Colorado, 2000.

————. "Our Lady of Guadelupe, Gift of a Loving God." Faith & Leadership. December 5, 2011. https://faithandleadership.com/virgilio-elizondo-our-lady-guadalupe-gift-loving-god.

"Essential Oils in the Ancient World: Part II." *The Lavender Life* (blog), Young Living Essential Oils, April 15, 2015. https://www.youngliving.com/blog/essential-oils-in-the-ancient-world-part-ii/.

Evans, Rachel Held. *Inspired: Slaying Giants, Walking on Water, and Loving the Bible Again.* Nashville: Thomas Nelson, 2018.

————. *Searching for Sunday: Loving, Leaving, and Finding the Church.* Nashville: Nelson Books, 2015.

Fallas, Amy. "In the Garden of Eden with Shakira." *Sojourners,* February 7, 2020. https://sojo.net/articles/garden-eden-shakira.

Fernandez, Manny. "'You Have to Pay with Your Body': The Hidden Nightmare of Sexual Violence on the Border." *The New York Times.* March 3, 2019. https://www.nytimes.com/2019/03/03/us/border-rapes-migrant-women.html.

Fernández, Stephanie. "Celia Cruz's 'Son Con Guaguancó' and the Bridge to Fame in Exile." *NPR*. February 13, 2018. https://www.npr.org/2018/02/13/584004511/celia-cruzs-son-con-guaguanc-and-the-bridge-to-fame-in-exile.

Fernández-Albán, Ary. *Decolonizing Theology in Revolution: A Critical Retrieval of Sergio Arce's Theological Thought*. Cham, Switzerland: Palgrave Macmillan, 2018.

Figueroa, Maria. "Toward a Spiritual Pedagogy along the Borderlands." In *Fleshing the Spirit: Spirituality and Activism in Chicana, Latina, and Indigenous Women's Lives*, edited by Elisa Facló and Irene Lara, 34–42. Tucson: University of Arizona Press, 2014.

Fiorenza, Elisabeth Schüssler. *But She Said: Feminist Practices of Biblical Interpretation*. Boston: Beacon, 1992.

Frymer-Kensky, Tikva. "Saviors of the Exodus." In *Reading the Women of the Bible: A New Interpretation of Their Stories*, 24–33. New York: Schocken, 2002.

Fuchs, Esther. "Status and Role of Female Heroines in the Biblical Narrative." In Bach, *Women in the Hebrew Bible*, 77–84.

Gafney, Wilda. "When Gomer Looks More like God." *The Rev. Wil Gafney, Ph.D.* (blog). September 24, 2018. https://www.wilgafney.com/2018/09/24/when-gomer-looks-more-like-god/.

———. *Womanist Midrash: A Reintroduction to the Women of the Torah and the Throne*. Louisville: Westminster John Knox, 2017.

Garcia, Mario T., ed. *The Gospel of César Chávez: My Faith in Action*. Celebrating Faith. Lanham, MD: Sheed & Ward, 2007.

García-Alfonso, Cristina. *Resolviendo: Narratives of Survival in the Hebrew Bible and in Cuba Today*. New York: Peter Lang, 2010.

García-Johnson, Oscar. *Spirit Outside the Gate: Decolonial Pneumatologies of the American Global South*. Missiological Engagements. Downers Grove, IL: IVP Academic, 2019.

García-Rivera, Alejandro. *The Community of the Beautiful: A Theological Aesthetics*. Collegeville, MN: Liturgical Press, 1999.

Gemi-Iordanou, Effie, Stephen Gordon, Robert Matthew, and Ellen McInnes. *Medicine, Healing and Performance*. Oxford: Oxbow Books, 2014.

Gibbs, Charlotte Mitchell. *Household Textiles*. Boston: Whitcomb & Barrows, 1912.

González, Justo L. *Mañana: Christian Theology from a Hispanic Perspective.* Nashville: Abingdon, 1990.

González, Karen. *The God Who Sees: Immigrants, the Bible, and the Journey to Belong.* Harrisonburg, VA: Herald, 2019.

Gonzalez, Michelle A. *Afro-Cuban Theology: Religion, Race, Culture, and Identity.* Gainesville: University Press of Florida, 2006.

Gossai, Hemchand, ed. *Postcolonial Commentary and the Old Testament.* New York: T&T Clark, 2019.

Guardiola-Sáenz, Leticia A. "Border-Crossing and Its Redemptive Power in John 7.53–8.11: A Cultural Reading of Jesus and the *Accused*." In *John and Postcolonialism: Travel, Space, and Power,* edited by M. W. Dube and J. L. Staley, 129–52. New York: Sheffield Academic, 2002.

Gutiérrez, Gustavo. *We Drink from Our Own Wells: The Spiritual Journey of a People.* 20th anniv. ed. Maryknoll, NY: Orbis Books, 2003.

Hall, William J., Mimi V. Chapman, Kent M. Lee, Yesenia M. Merino, Tainayah W. Thomas, B. Keith Payne, Eugenia Eng, Steven H. Day, and Tamera Coyne-Beasley. "Implicit Racial/Ethnic Bias among Health Care Professionals and Its Influence on Health Care Outcomes: A Systematic Review." *American Journal of Public Health* 105, no. 12 (December 2015): e60–e76. https://www.ncbi.nlm.nih.gov/pmc/articles/PMC4638275/.

Hamori, Esther J. *Women's Divination in Biblical Literature: Prophecy, Necromancy, and Other Arts of Knowledge.* New Haven: Yale University Press, 2015.

Hasan Al-Saidi, Afaf Ahmed. "Post-colonialism Literature the Concept of *Self* and the *Other* in Coetzee's *Waiting for the Barbarians*: An Analytical Approach." *Journal of Language Teaching and Research* 5, no. 1 (2014): 95–105.

Hidalgo, Jacqueline M. *Revelation in Aztlán: Scriptures, Utopias, and the Chicano Movement.* The Bible and Cultural Studies. New York: Palgrave Macmillan, 2016.

Honig, Bonnie. "Ruth, the Model Emigrée: Mourning and the Symbolic Politics of Immigration." In Brenner, *Ruth and Esther,* 50–74.

Isasi-Díaz, Ada María. "Mujerista Discourse: A Platform for Latinas' Subjugated Knowledge." In *Decolonizing Epistemologies: Latina/o Theology and Philosophy,* edited by Ada María Isasi-Díaz and Eduardo Mendieta, 44–67. Transdisciplinary Theological Colloquia. New York: Fordham University Press, 2012.

————. *Mujerista Theology: A Theology for the Twenty-First Century*. Maryknoll, NY: Orbis Books, 1996.

Isasi-Díaz, Ada María, and Fernando F. Segovia, eds. *Hispanic/Latino Theology: Challenge and Promise*. Minneapolis: Fortress, 1996.

Jackson, Melissa A. *Comedy and Feminist Interpretation of the Hebrew Bible: A Subversive Collaboration*. Oxford Theological Monographs. Oxford: Oxford University Press, 2012.

Jaramillo, Juliana Jiménez. "The Queasy Cultural Legacy of *Sábado Gigante*." Brow Beat, *Slate*, April 21, 2015. https://slate.com/culture/2015/04/sabado-gigante-canceled-all-spanish-speakers-should-be-glad-it-s-finally-going-off-the-air.html.

Jennings, Willie James. *After Whiteness: A Theological Education in Belonging*. Grand Rapids: Eerdmans, 2020.

————. "Can 'White' People Be Saved: Reflections on Missions and Whiteness." Speech given as part of the Fuller Dialogues: Race and Identity. Posted by Fuller Studio on February 24, 2018. https://fullerstudio.fuller.edu/fuller-dialogues-race-theology-and-mission/.

————. *The Christian Imagination: Theology and the Origins of Race*. New Haven: Yale University Press, 2010.

"John MacArthur Beth Moore Go Home." Reformation Charlotte. October 18, 2019. YouTube video, 7:35. https://www.youtube.com/watch?v=NeNKHqpBcgc.

Jones, Barry. "The Oldest Trick in the Book: Narrative Explorations of Oppression and Resistance in Exodus 1." *Review & Expositor* 114 (2017): 157–65.

Kam, Rose. *Their Stories, Our Stories: Women of the Bible*. New York: Continuum, 1995.

Keegan, William F., and Lisabeth A. Carlson. *Talking Taíno: Caribbean Natural History from a Native Perspective*. Tuscaloosa: University of Alabama Press, 2008.

Keener, Craig. *Acts: An Exegetical Commentary*. Vol. 2, *3:1–14:28*. Grand Rapids: Baker Academic, 2013.

————. *A Commentary on the Gospel of Matthew*. Grand Rapids: Eerdmans, 1999.

Klein, Lillian R. "Achsah, What Price This Prize?" In Brenner, *Judges*, 18–26.

————. "Hannah: Marginalized Victim and Social Redeemer." In Brenner, *Samuel and Kings*, 77–92.

Kohles, Sarah. "Euodia, Syntyche, and Lydia: The Leading Ladies of Philippi in Philippians 4:2–3 and Acts 16:11–15, 40." PhD diss., Catholic Theological Union at Chicago, 2015. Theological Research Exchange Network.

Kohn, Natalia, Noemi Vega Quiñones, and Kristy Garza Robinson. *Hermanas: Deepening Our Identity and Growing Our Influence.* Downers Grove, IL: InterVarsity, 2018.

Kramer, Phyllis Silverman. "Miriam." In Brenner, *Exodus to Deuteronomy*, 104–33. Sheffield: Sheffield Academic, 2000.

Kreps, Daniel. "Nipple Ripples: 10 Years of Fallout from Janet Jackson's Halftime Show." Culture, *Rolling Stone*, January 30, 2014. https://www.rollingstone.com/culture/culture-news/nipple-ripples-10-years-of-fallout-from-janet-jacksons-halftime-show-122792/.

Kwok, Pui-lan, ed. *Hope Abundant: Third World and Indigenous Women's Theology.* Maryknoll, NY: Orbis Books, 2010.

Labberton, Mark. "Willie James Jennings on Race." Posted February 14, 2017. *Conversing.* Podcast, 01:04:06. https://conversing.libsyn.com/6-willie-james-jennings-on-race.

Lapsley, Jacqueline. *Whispering the Word: Hearing Women's Stories in the Old Testament.* Louisville: Westminster John Knox, 2005.

Leahy, Anna. "What Does It Mean to Live with a Body That Can't Be Fixed?" *BuzzFeed News.* September 28, 2018. https://www.buzzfeednews.com/article/annaleahy/living-with-chronic-pain-that-cant-be-fixed-ada-limon.

Lee, Hak Joon. *We Will Get to the Promised Land: Martin Luther King, Jr.'s Communal-Political Spirituality.* Eugene, OR: Wipf & Stock, 2017.

Leseho, Johanna, and Lisa Rene Maxwell. "Coming Alive: Creative Movement as a Personal Coping Strategy on the Path to Healing and Growth." *British Journal of Guidance & Counseling* 38, no. 1 (February 2010): 17–30.

Levine, Amy-Jill, and Marc Zvi Brettler, eds. *The Jewish Annotated New Testament: New Revised Standard Version Bible Translation.* New York: Oxford University Press, 2011.

Lewis, Jone Johnson. "35 Zora Neale Hurston Quotes." ThoughtCo. December 9, 2019. https://www.thoughtco.com/zora-neale-hurston-quotes-3530194.

Limón, Ada. "Wonder Woman." In *The Carrying: Poems*, 42. Minneapolis: Milkweed Editions, 2018.

Loera-Brus, Antonio, de. "Latinos Owe African Americans Everything." *The Tennessee Tribune.* August 5, 2020. https://tntribune.com/latinos -owe-african-americans-everything/.

Lopez, Juan Carlos, and Rogelio Robles. "Latina Evangélicas Panel Discussion [with Dr. Elizabeth Conde-Frazier]." Posted November 7, 2017. *Spanglish Seminary Podcast.* 97:00. https://www.stitcher.com/show /spanglish-seminary/episode/latina-evangelicas-panel-discussion-with -dr-elizabeth-conde-frazier-52152628.

Love, Stuart. *Jesus and Marginal Women: The Gospel of Matthew in Social-Scientific Perspective.* Eugene, OR: Cascade Books, 2009.

Markham, Clements R. *The Journal of Christopher Columbus (During His First Voyage, 1492–93): And Documents Relating to the Voyages of John Cabot and Gaspar Corte Real.* Farnham, UK: Hakluyt Society, 2010.

Martell-Otero, Loida I., Zaida Maldonado Pérez, and Elizabeth Conde-Frazier. *Latina Evangélicas: A Theological Survey from the Margins.* Eugene, OR: Cascade Books, 2013.

McCaulley, Esau. *Reading While Black: African American Biblical Interpretation as an Exercise in Hope.* Downers Grove, IL: InterVarsity, 2020.

McSherry, J. Patrice. "Operation Condor: Clandestine Inter-American System." *Social Justice* 26, no. 4 (1999): 144–74.

Medina, Lara, and Martha R. Gonzales, eds. *Voices from the Ancestors: Xicanx and Latinx Spiritual Expressions and Healing Practices.* Tucson: University of Arizona Press, 2019.

Mehta, Angeli. "Beyond Recycling: Putting the Brakes on Fast Fashion." *Reuters Events,* April 28, 2019. https://www.reutersevents.com/sustain ability/beyond-recycling-putting-brakes-fast-fashion.

Menchú, Rigoberta, and Elisabeth Burgos-Debray. *I, Rigoberta Menchú: An Indian Woman in Guatemala.* London: Verso, 2009. Ebook.

Mendes, Karla. "Resisting to Exist: Indigenous Women Unite against Brazil's Far-Right President." *Amazon Watch,* May 20, 2019. https://amazon watch.org/news/2019/0520-resisting-to-exist.

Meyers, Carol. "The Family in Early Israel." In *Families in Ancient Israel,* by Leo G. Perdue, Joseph Blenkinsopp, John J. Collins, and Carol Meyers, 1–47. The Family, Religion, and Culture. Louisville: Westminster John Knox, 1997.

———. "Hannah and Her Sacrifice: Reclaiming Female Agency." In Brenner, *Samuel and Kings,* 93–105.

————. "The Hannah Narrative in Feminist Perspective." In *Go to the Land I Will Show You: Studies in Honor of Dwight W. Young*, edited by Dwight W. Young, Joseph E. Coleson, Victor Harold Matthews, and Joseph Coleson, 117–26. Winona Lake, IN: Eisenbrauns, 1996.

————. *Households and Holiness: The Religious Culture of Israelite Women.* Facets. Minneapolis: Fortress, 2005.

————. "Returning Home: Ruth 1.8 and the Gendering of the Book of Ruth." In Brenner, *Ruth and Esther*, 85–114.

Mignolo, Walter. *Local Histories/Global Designs: Coloniality, Subaltern Knowledges, and Border Thinking.* Princeton Studies in Culture/Power/History. Princeton: Princeton University Press, 2012.

Missing and Murdered: Confronting the Silent Crisis in Indian Country, before the Committee on Indian Affairs, United States Senate. December 12, 2018. Testimony of Charles Addington, director – Office of Justice Services, Bureau of Indian Affairs. https://www.doi.gov/ocl/indian-country-crisis.

Morrison, Aaron. "Here's Everything You Need to Know about the Mothers of the Movement." *Mic*, July 26, 2016. https://www.mic.com/articles/149802/here-s-everything-you-need-to-know-about-the-mothers-of-the-movement.

"Mother Teresa Reflects on Working Toward World Peace." Architects of Peace. Accessed January 12, 2021. https://www.scu.edu/mcae/architects-of-peace/Teresa/essay.html.

Moulds, Josephine. "Child Labour in the Fashion Supply Chain: Where, Why, and What Can Be Done." *The Guardian*. Accessed February 6, 2021. https://labs.theguardian.com/unicef-child-labour/.

Muñoz, Susana Blaustein, and Lourdes Portillo, dirs. *The Mothers of Plaza De Mayo* (documentary). 1985; Buenos Aires, Argentina: Women Make Movies, 1985.

Mutchler, J. E., L. A. Baker, and S. Lee. "Grandparents Responsible for Grandchildren in Native-American Families." *Social Science Quarterly* 88, no. 4 (2007): 990–1009.

Newsom, Carol A., Sharon H. Ringe, and Jacqueline E. Lapsley, eds. *Women's Bible Commentary*. 3rd ed. Louisville: Westminster John Knox, 2012.

Nikondeha, Kelley. *Defiant: What the Women of Exodus Teach Us about Freedom.* Grand Rapids: Eerdmans, 2020.

Norton, Yolanda. "Silenced Struggles for Survival: Finding Life in Death in the Book of Ruth." In M. Smith, *I Found God in Me*, 266–80.

O'Day, Gail R. "The Gospel of John: Introduction, Commentary and Reflections." In *Luke–John*, edited by Leander E. Keck, 496–865. Vol. 9 of *The New Interpreter's Bible*. Nashville: Abingdon, 1994.

Osborne, Grant R., and Clinton E. Arnold. *Matthew*. Zondervan Exegetical Commentary Series: New Testament 1. Grand Rapids: Zondervan, 2010.

Pedraza, Sylvia. "Los Marielitos of 1980: Race, Class, Gender, and Sexuality." ACSE Cuba. November 30, 2004. https://www.ascecuba.org/asce _proceedings/los-marielitos-of-1980-race-class-gender-and-sexuality/.

Penner, Louis A., Irene V. Blair, Terrance L. Albrecht, and John F. Dovidio. "Reducing Racial Health Care Disparities: A Social Psychological Analysis." *Policy Insights from the Behavioral and Brain Sciences* 1, no. 1 (October 2014): 204–12. https://www.ncbi.nlm.nih.gov/pmc/articles /PMC4332703/.

Peterson, Eugene. *The Word Made Flesh: The Language of Jesus in His Stories and Prayers*. London: Hodder & Stoughton, 2008.

Pinto-Bailey, Cristina Ferreira, and Maria Firmina dos Reis. "'The Slave Woman': An Introduction." *Afro-Hispanic Review* 32, no. 1 (Spring 2013): 205–18. www.jstor.org/stable/23617266.

Ramsey, K. J. *This Too Shall Last: Finding Grace When Suffering Lingers*. Grand Rapids: Zondervan, 2020.

"The Rana Plaza Accident and Its Aftermath." International Labour Organization. Accessed February 6, 2021. https://www.ilo.org/global/topics /geip/WCMS_614394/lang--en/index.htm.

Reid, Barbara E. "A Godly Widow Persistently Pursuing Justice: Luke 18:1–8." *Biblical Research* 45 (2000): 25–33.

Reyes, Patrick B. *Nobody Cries When We Die: God, Community, and Surviving to Adulthood*. Nashville: Chalice, 2016. ProQuest Ebook Central.

Rivera, Mayra. "God at the Crossroads: A Postcolonial Reading of Sophia." In *The Postcolonial Biblical Reader*, edited by R. S. Sugirtharajah. Oxford: Wiley & Sons, 2005. ProQuest Ebook Central.

Robinson, Jo Ann. *The Montgomery Bus Boycott and the Women Who Started It: The Memoir of Jo Ann Gibson Robinson*. Edited by David J. Garrow. Knoxville: University of Tennessee Press, 1987.

Rodríguez, Jeanette, and Ted Fortier. *Cultural Memory: Resistance, Faith, and Identity*. Austin: University of Texas Press, 2007.

Romero, Robert Chao. *Brown Church: Five Centuries of Latina/o Social Justice, Theology, and Identity*. Downers Grove, IL: InterVarsity, 2020.

————. "The Spiritual Praxis of Cesar Chavez." *Hispanic Theological Initiative/Perspectivas* (Princeton Theological Seminary) (2017): 24–39.

Ruether, Rosemary Radford. *Sexism and God-Talk: Toward a Feminist Theology; With a New Introduction*. Twentieth Century Religious Thought. Boston: Beacon, 1993.

Sacks, Jonathan. *Rabbi Jonathan Sack's Haggadah: Hebrew and English Text with New Essays and Commentary*. Jerusalem: Maggid Books, 2015.

Saldaña, Ruben Jr. "Orale! Food and Identity Amongst Latinos." *Institute for Latino Studies* (University of Notre Dame) 6, no. 4 (2001): 1–10.

Samulowitz, Anke, Ida Gremyr, Erik Eriksson, and Gunnel Hensing. "'Brave Men' and 'Emotional Women': A Theory-Guided Literature Review on Gender Bias in Health Care and Gender Norms towards Patients with Chronic Pain." *Pain Research and Management* 2018 (February 25, 2018): 1–14. https://doi.org/10.1155/2018/6358624.

Santos, Boaventura de Sousa. *Epistemologies of the South: Justice against Epistemicide*. New York: Taylor & Francis Group, 2014.

Serano, Julia. *Excluded: Making Feminsist and Queer Movements More Inclusive*. Berkely, CA: Seal, 2013.

Siegal, William. *Aymara-Bolivianische Textilien*. Krefeld: Deutsches Textilmuseum, 1991.

Smith, George Adam. *Historical Geography of the Holy Land: Especially in Relation to the History of Israel and of the Early Church*. 15th ed. New York: Hodder & Stoughton, 1896.

Smith, Mitzi J., ed. *I Found God in Me: A Womanist Biblical Hermeneutics Reader*. Eugene, OR: Cascade Books, 2015.

Spalding, Diana. "When George Floyd Called Out for His Mama, Mothers Everywhere Answered." *Motherly*, June 4, 2020. https://www.mother.ly/news/george-floyd-called-for-mothers-everywhere.

Stevenson, Bryan. *Just Mercy: A Story of Justice and Redemption*. New York: Spiegel & Grau, 2014.

Stringer, Tracey. "Hannah: More than a Mother." *Priscilla Papers* 33, no.1, (2019): 3–6.

Thurman, Howard. *Jesus and the Disinherited*. Boston: Beacon, 1996.

Tinker, George E. *Spirit and Resistance: Political Theology and American Indian Liberation*. Minneapolis: Fortress, 2004. Kindle.

Tippett, Krista. "Robin Wall Kimmerer: The Intelligence of Plants." Aired February 25, 2016, updated August 20, 2020. *On Being with Krista Tippett*. Podcast, 50:55. https://onbeing.org/programs/robin-wall-kimmerer -the-intelligence-of-plants/.

Trible, Phyllis. "A Human Comedy: The Book of Ruth." In *Literary Interpretations of Biblical Narratives*. Vol. 2, edited by Kenneth R. R. Gros Louis with James S. Ackerman, 161–90. Nashville: Abingdon, 1982.

Tweed, Thomas A. *Our Lady of the Exile: Diasporic Religion at a Cuban Catholic Shrine in Miami*. Religion in America Series. New York: Oxford University Press, 1997.

UN General Assembly. Resolution 61/295. United Nations Declaration on the Rights of Indigenous Peoples. September 13, 2007. https://www.un .org/development/desa/indigenouspeoples/wp-content/uploads/sites /19/2018/11/UNDRIP_E_web.pdf.

Van der Kolk, Bessel A. *The Body Keeps the Score: Brain, Mind, and Body in the Healing of Trauma*. New York: Penguin Books, 2015.

"Walter Mignolo 'Colonial Wounds, Decolonial Healing.'" Sharing Life. May 22, 2019. Vimeo video, 1:03:15. https://vimeo.com/337899001.

Warrior, Robert Allen. "Canaanites, Cowboys, and Indians: Deliverance, Conquest, and Liberation Theology Today." *Christianity and Crisis* 49, no. 12 (1989): 21–26.

Weems, Renita J. "'The Hebrew Women Are Not Like the Egyptian Women: The Ideology of Race, Gender and Sexual Reproduction in Exodus 1." *Semeia* 59 (1992): 25–34.

Witherington, Benjamin, III. "Joanna: Apostle of the Lord—or Jailbait?" *Bible Review* 21, no. 2 (2005): 12–14.

Yoshinori, Kamo. "Asian Grandparents." In *Handbook on Grandparenthood*, edited by Maximiliane E. Szinovácz, 97–112. Westport, CT: Greenwood, 1998.

Yugar, Theresa A. *Sor Juana Inés de la Cruz: Feminist Reconstruction of Biography and Text*. Eugene, OR: Wipf & Stock, 2014.

Zaru, Jean. "Biblical Teachings and the Hard Realities of Life." In Kwok, *Hope Abundant*, 123–37.

Zinn, Howard. *A People's History of the United States: 1492–Present*. Harper Perennial Modern Classics. New York: HarperPerennial, 2005. Ebook.